Training with Cerutty

by Larry Myers

World Publications
Box 366, Mountain View, CA 94042

World Publications
Box 366, Mountain View, CA 94042

ISBN 0-89037-080x (Hb) -081-8 (Pb)
Library of Congress 77-85377

This book is graciously dedicated to Percy and Nancy Cerutty, Ben "Pops" Keane and all of the light-hearted chaps from all over the world who have made their pilgrimage to Portsea, Australia.

Acknowledgements

Many people throughout the world of track and field sent me their photos for this book so that it would be an International textbook of training.

I wish to thank the following: *Australia:* Percy Wells Cerutty, Director of the International Health, Athletic and Fitness Centre, Portsea, Victoria; L. (Jess) Jarver, editor of *Modern Athlete and Coach,* Adelaide, South Australia; Leslie Perry, Honorary Secretary of the Ringwood Harriers, Ringwood East, Victoria; *Czechoslovakia:* Alfred Janecky, editor of *Athletika,* Prague; *Eastern Germany:* Herbert Pilzecker, editor of *ADN-Zentralbild,* East Berlin; *France:* Alain Mimoun of Champigny Sur Marne; *Great Britain*: Rachel Hackenschmidt and Bill Lofberg of London; *Italy:* Roberto Quercetani, author of many fine athletic books, Firenze; *The Netherlands*: Nic. L. Lemmens, editor of *De Athletiekwereld,* Waalre; *New Zealand*: Bill Baillie of Mt. Rosebill; *The United States*: Ted Corbitt of the New York Pioneer Club; Raymond G. Lumpp, athletic director of the New York Athletic Club; Cordner Nelson, publisher of *Track and Field News*, Los Altos, Calif.; Mike O'Hara, president of the International Track Association, Los Angeles, Calif.; Jim Ryun of Santa Barbara, Calif.; Frank Shorter of Boulder, Colo.; *Western Germany*: Lutz D. Nebenthal, Press Manager of *Deutscher Leichtathletik Verband,* Darmstadt; Toni Nett, Olympic and IAAF photographer, *Wurtingen.*

The photos of Percy Cerutty running were contributed by David H. Clarke of Glen Ellyn, Ill. Percy Cerutty's lecture on the five basic movements was transcribed from a series of tape recordings that Bruce V. Guthrie, Napa, Calif., made during his visit to Portsea in December, 1970.

Contents

Foreword

In the 12 months that Larry Myers spent at the International Health, Athletic and Fitness Center in Portsea, he was able to learn my techniques and philosophy better than anyone ever had before. Herb Elliott was the athlete who understood my ideas best, and Larry Myers was the academician who best grasped them. He spent hundreds of hours poring through my more than 1000 textbooks on all aspects of medicine and health.

He learned that running well requires more than just natural ability and large quantities of physical training. It involves a totally different approach to *movement*. Running in the orthodox fashion, especially on long runs of 10 or 20 miles each day, destroys the athlete's inherent speed. It ruins all spontaneity of movement and turns the runner into a robot, instead of freeing his mind and body so that he can become a first-class athlete.

The top athletes of the future must learn the five basic movements that are outlined in this book. They must learn the proper diet and they must do resistance training, both with weights and by running through sand. All of my 30 world record-breakers over the past 23 years ran up sand hills in practice.

Most importantly, the athlete of the future must learn how to fully fill his lungs. The top runners today run with their elbows locked in one movement.

This does not allow them to fill even a quarter of the upper lobes of their lungs.

Herb Elliott was able to knock 20 seconds off his mile time and become a world-class miler after only a little more than a year of my training. When these techniques are understood and developed by coaches and athletes all over the world, there will be a new set of records in every track and field event.

Now that I am 80 years old, I have finished teaching the young athletes to run. I now pass this role to Larry Myers, because he can teach the proper ways of movement, so today's runners can set the world records of the future.

Percy Wells Cerutty
The International Athletic Center
Portsea, Australia

Introduction

It is my goal that this book will be a guiding light to athletes all over the world. This is an international textbook that any athlete or coach can use. This book fills the gap of most athletic books because it brings the mind and body together in complete harmony with the forces of nature and the universe.

The proper neural pattern is the one element in the athlete's training routine that links the mind to any part of the body. In track and field (and distance running), the athlete's neural pattern is the one factor that will make the difference between victory or defeat.

It is very important that the reader grasps the basic concepts of this book so that he can channel his mind to fulfill his own destiny and goals in athletics.

The mere fact that you are reading this book means that there is a golden spark of greatness in you that beckons to be developed to its full potential. The important question is: How much do you wish to excel in your event? For many athletes, there is no limit. Every person has a spark of greatness, and the outcome of his athletic goals is determined by the path he decides to take to develop his mental and physical gifts. This book is designed to make the development more fulfilling.

It is highly recommended that the reader only use the training schedules as a guide, altering them to suit his individual requirements. The person's daily training schedule should fit his own strengths and weaknesses. In short, no athlete should ever be a slave to any training schedule printed in an athletic textbook.

The training year for any athlete in the world who is using this book to excel in his chosen event will be divided up into three training periods: the conditioning period (six months), the practice period (three months) and the competition period over the last three months of his athletic year.

If the athlete lives in the northern hemisphere, he would use the following programs:

● *Conditioning Period* (6 months): high school and college—July through December; World Class—September through February;

● *Practice Period* (3 months): high school and college—January through March; World Class—March through May.

● *Competition Period* (3 months): high school and college—April through June; World Class—June through August.

If the athlete lives in the southern hemisphere, where the seasons are reversed, he would follow this program.

● *Conditioning Period* (6 months): high school and college—April through September; World Class—June throught November.

● *Practice Period* (3 months): high school and college—October through December; World Class—December through February.

● *Competition Period* (3 months): high school and college—January through March; World Class—March through May.

The world class runner's training year is extended further into the summer months because these athletes have more track meets later on in the summer than the high school or college athlete.

The training schedules are only guides, like road maps, to the athlete's final destination down the highway of success and jubilation. They get the athlete on the proper road to success so he can achieve his full potential.

Percy Cerutty said, "I always encourage the athletes who come to Portsea to be independent in their training. This can only be accomplished when the person makes his own schedule each day in terms of what he wants to accomplish during his life. When any coach gives a schedule to an athlete, it seems to take all the fun out of athletics. I only counsel the athlete who seeks my help on running technique, or asks me to evaluate his training diary. Every athlete should keep an accurate training diary with all his workouts so he will know where he has been in the course of his training road and where he can plan to go in the future to be one step closer to his goals.

"Here at Portsea, I only demonstrate what the athlete must do to get to the very top of the world in his event, and then the person decides how much work he must do in order to achieve his goals. I never plan training schedules for athletes. When the athlete makes his own training schedules each day, this is a sign of independence that is a mark of a true champion."

Shortly before the completion of this book, Percy Cerutty died at his home in Portsea after a brief illness. This book will carry on the torch for him, and I am sure it will reach the hands of the world record-holder of the future.

Larry Myers
Denver, Colo.

I

THE CERUTTY SYSTEM

1

Percy Cerutty's Life

If not for a case of double pneumonia when he was six years old, Percy Cerutty might never have developed his controversial running style. The ailment caused partial paralysis of his left lung and for many years created discomfort whenever he ran.

What would have made a normal person avoid running only served to spawn a lifelong interest with Cerutty. He became determined to discover an alternate, less painful way of running.

Born in the working-class Melbourne suburb of Prahran on Jan. 10, 1895, Cerutty ran, and won, his first race in 1913. It was a one-mile run. Between 1913 and 1918, he ran 36 distance races, winning 10 of them.

From an early age, he sensed that animals, particularly wild animals, moved much more naturally and efficiently than man. He grew up around horses and spent a great deal of time watching and studying them. When he imitated their movements, he found not only that he ran with less pain from his lung, but also that he ran more efficiently, utilizing oxygen more effectively.

Many years later, tracing the development of his ideas, Percy said, "I have learned more from watching race horses than from any runner I've seen in any Olympic Games."

His new style of running developed in part at the Caulfield Race Course, in Australia, where he would regularly observe the movement of horses and then

Cerutty proudly displays his Member of the British Empire award presented by Queen Elizabeth.

emulate them on his way home. It's no mystery where the terms "trot," "canter" and "gallop," three of Cerutty's most famous running techniques, came from.

His study of animal movement soon went beyond horses, as he found that there was something to be learned from each species of animal.

He observed how anthropoid apes ran in an effortless shuffle, without high knee lifts in front or kick-ups in back. As the ape moved, he threw his arms and shoulders forward, plagued neither with shoulder sway or locked elbows (both of which are characteristic of human movement).

Cerutty studied the antelope and gazelle, observing how they utilized nervous energy and how they managed to run *over* the ground instead of on it. This later had a great effect on his views about sprinters and hurdlers. He saw that animals had a tremendous sense of balance, which humans lacked, but which if applied to running, sprinting and hurdling in particular, could lead to new plateaus of development.

Although Percy saw that civilized man had practically none of this sort of movement, when he visited primitive tribes, he was surprised to find that they possessed much of the same natural motion of wild animals.

After making periodic visits to observe the unspoiled Australian Aborigine, he concluded that if not for the constant negative training imposed on civilized man almost from birth, he too would move in this natural manner.

The confirmation came when he found a link between primitive man and another species of animal: the human child. Young children were the only form of civilized man who ran in a natural, uninhibited manner. Unfortunately, by the time they began grade school, this natural movement was invariably denied by parents and regimented physical education programs.

"All primitives instinctively 'toe-in' when they walk," said Cerutty. "In modern civilization, young children instinctively 'toe-in' from birth until they are reprimanded by their parents and school teachers who teach them to point their feet to the side when they walk. This is unnatural and ruins the uninhibited gift of movement we are given at birth."

Young children run naturally, he found, without the locked elbows typical of top athletes.

Discovery of this link both fascinated and disturbed Cerutty. He would watch with great interest the play of pre-schoolers, amazed at their endurance. Invariably, if they were really enjoying what they were doing, the young could push themselves relentlessly. They could go on for hours.

Utilizing the principles learned from the play of children was a key in Cerutty's running theories. "The child is the father of the adult," he was fond of saying. In terms of movement, what the adult could learn from the child was much more valuable than what the child could learn from the adult.

A lifetime of observation and contemplation turned to experimentation and application when Cerutty was 46. At 43, he lost his job as an Australian civil servant because of an unspecified illness that drained the strength from his movement and caused a tremendous loss of weight. He later found that this illness resulted from his migraine headaches.

When Cerutty had a migraine attack, he would go down to the Caulfield Race Course to watch his favorite racehorse Ajax, go through a workout. Watching the horse circle the track eased the tensions. When Percy was through looking at the horse gallop, he went back home emulating Ajax. Percy said, "Ajax put more spirit and life into me than anyone I have ever known! No wonder I often say that I prefer most horses, dogs and snakes to all people!"

When his condition worsened to the point that doctors feared for his life, Percy's will to live got the better of him. He began running again, more seriously than ever before.

He would take long, solitary walks, thinking about ways of applying what he had learned about human movement to himself. This was difficult because it involved both learning and *relearning*.

Actually, the "new" training was a return to the movements a child makes; the natural movement that growing up takes away.

This process was obviously difficult to perfect. But he believed that if it was done faithfully, in a step-by-step manner, almost anything could be learned. His end goal was to make the child-like freedom of movement part of the adult again.

He was also intrigued with the idea of being able to ignore pain. He remembered how remarkable it had seemed when the sound barrier was broken. He thought it would be much more remarkable if we could break the *pain* barrier. He realized that part of this barrier wasn't really pain but just fear of pain.

George Hackenschmidt helped Cerutty crystalize his athletic philosophy and techniques.

He wondered what it would be like to run without the barriers of fear, guilt and anxiety that were conditioned in the athlete's mind, causing nervous inhibitions. This stopped the mind and body from flowing in a spontaneous manner, like animals.

When he reached his mid-50s, though, he sensed that for the true fulfillment of this idea, he would need a younger athlete, one who had suffered less "programming," who was still able to adapt the child-like movement without a great deal of difficulty.

He began seriously working with other athletes when he was 55. He started his famous training camp by the sea at Portsea, first only on weekends but eventually as a full-time operation.

His racing also stopped at this point, but his conditioning and training never did. At the age of 62, seven years after he stopped competing, he ran the mile in 5:32.5 and just a quarter of an hour later ran two miles in 13 minutes. At the age of 70, he could still break six minutes in the mile.

"If you have a talent, it's almost criminal to waste it," Herb Elliott wrote. "He himself has tried to excel in several spheres, but he realized he was going to wind up a non-entity in the post office, he became bored by politics (he was once a member of the Trades Hall), and he lacked the physique to be a champion athlete. He did not become happy until his success as a coach. He excels as a coach and he tells all his pupils that they also must not settle for anything unless they know that one day they will excel in it."

It was after the 1956 Melbourne Olympics that 18-year-old Herb Elliott first came to Portsea. His best mile time was then only 4:20, and for the past year he had not run at all. But a visit to the Olympics inspired him, and he was anxious to run again.

Cerutty immediately was amazed at the dedication and determination Elliott displayed. He worked with him full-time, at Portsea on the weekends and in a large park and garden area in South Yarra the rest of the week. Although he had Elliott training as many as three times a day, none of it was around a track. It was all through parks, woods, beaches and golf courses.

"To me," Elliott wrote, "Percy's own life, his own struggle for achievement in the face of depressing handicaps, posed a challenge. With limited physical resources, he's courageously whipped himself to perform almost frighteningly athletic feats. I reckoned that if I didn't try to punish my young strong body as he did his older body, I'd despise myself."

Many other athletes trained with Cerutty during this time, but none applied themselves as Elliott did. When he was 18, Herb cut his mile time down to 4:06, and less than two weeks after his 19th birthday, he ran 4:00.5.

As the training camp developed, Cerutty began to realize his goal of having adults acquire the neural patterns of children. All of the runners at Portsea lived a relatively communal existence. They ate together, napped together and played together—throwing each other into the ocean, wrestling on the beach, running through the sand. And, almost as a by-product of this play, they became efficient, top-caliber, athletes together.

Always stressing closeness to nature (long before it became a fad), Cerutty had his athletes on a diet of almost exclusively natural foods. He believed that the abundance of synthetic foods in modern society severely hampered an athlete's performance.

After the training camp became full-time, Percy made an observation that stabilized several of his

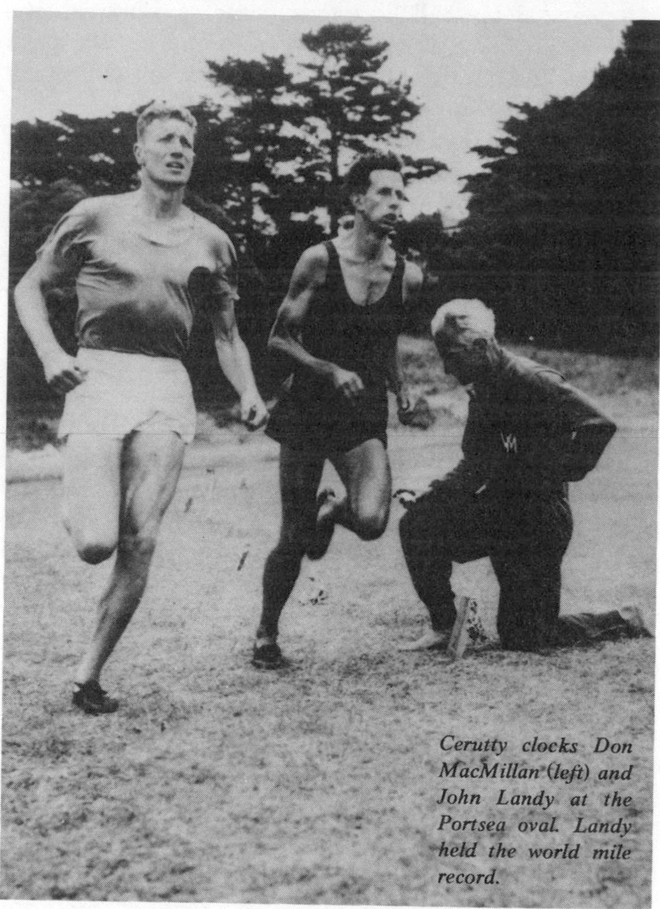

Cerutty clocks Don MacMillan (left) and John Landy at the Portsea oval. Landy held the world mile record.

views on running. It was something he would talk about for years. He was walking along a busy street with Elliott one afternoon when a man with no legs passed them on a roller board, his arms moving in a constant array of contortions.

Cerutty noticed several things about the man, each of which was implemented into his training program. What really caught his attention was the fact that the man was moving faster than everyone else. Percy sensed that the exaggerated movements of the man's arms were responsible for his speed and endurance, because they allowed more oxygen into his lungs.

He immediately related this to the varied arm movements of Emil Zatopek, winner of the three longest races at the 1952 Olympics. He also related it to his own technique of galloping like horses in order to force more oxygen into his lungs.

Another thing he observed in this man was the naturalness of his movement. His lack of legs gave him immunity to the unnatural movements the rest of the adult world suffered from. He moved more economically and much faster than the supposedly more fortunate members of mankind.

Percy was greatly impressed by the man's upper-body development. This contributed to his experimentation with weight lifting, and the eventual conclusion that it is a helpful aid for runners. He was always disturbed by the popular idea that weight training made athletes sluggish and muscle-bound. He found that, with runners, it did just the opposite. It gave them more overall strength, improved their reflexes, increased their endurance and lengthened their stride. Elliott worked with weights regularly.

The athlete who came to Cerutty had to make a total commitment to his ideas. The most important aspect of his methods was they they were more than just a way of training; they were a way of living. His philosophy was inseparable from his program. Many athletes were unable or unwilling to shed their unnatural movements, and drifted away. But those who remained became superb athletes.

"It's a startling fact that almost as many young men have deserted Percy as went AWOL in the last war," wrote Herb Elliott in 1960.

Elliott never lost a mile or 1500-meter race in his career. His world record 3:54.5 came in a race in which he wasn't pressed. He won a gold medal in the 1500 meters in world record time of 3:35.6 at the 1960 Olympics.

Other Cerutty-trained athletes included Dave Stephens, world record-holder in the six-mile, John Landy, world-class miler, and Albert Thomas, world record-holder in the two- and three-mile runs.

When Cerutty said that the athlete who fully utilized his ideas could run a 3:20 mile, he was talking of a total commitment, something that even some of his champions weren't giving. Many people have borrowed parts of Cerutty's ideas, but few have adopted them all, and none have on a permanent basis.

Elliott provided the major confirmation of Cerutty's theories. He was the athlete who best utilized his lungs and who had practically no shoulder sway. He developed this style through months of running behind Cerutty at Portsea. He was Percy's most successful athlete.

"He fulfilled my anticipations," Percy said many years later. "But today's athletes haven't followed up. If they used my techniques, they would be able to take up where Elliott left off. There are few milers today who can run as fast as Elliott did 15 years ago. And he was never beaten. If he had some of today's athletes to run against, he would have run even faster."

Percy Cerutty's life differed from most people's because he did more than just live it; he *used* it. He used it to study and experience all aspects of the world. He was a philosopher, a poet, an athlete and a coach. What repulsed him from an early age was how the majority of people went along with accepted

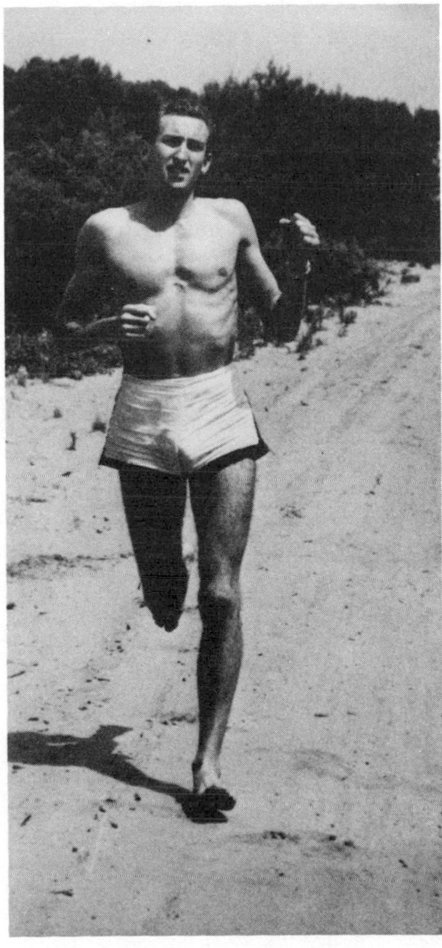

Herb Elliott, perhaps the greatest miler ever, takes a barefoot run on the sandy roads near Portsea.

notions, seldom bothering to question or even understand them. By the time they had formed a personality, they were nothing more than a collection of other people's ideas.

When Percy qualified me to carry on his ideas, he told me quite sincerely, "The day is coming in the near future when the four-minute mile will be as common as the 10-second 100-yard dash."

Although he believed the most profound effects would come in track and field, it has since had an impact on such champions as Margaret Court in tennis, Dawn Fraser in swimming and Jimmy Carruthers in boxing.

In the succeeding chapters, I will explain the specific ideas of Percy Cerutty. I believe they have a value for everyone, whether you are a top competitive athlete, or just a sometime recreational athlete. The major value of these ideas is that they all point toward a truer, more natural design for man. He always referred to adult man's movements as "zombie-like," and believed they led to a very restricted way of life. His ideas are all based on reversing this process. Their value is not just in improving athletic performance; it is in improving life.

2

Neural Patterns

I got involved with Percy Cerutty through a lengthy correspondence. Before I went to Portsea, I had been competing myself, as well as coaching athletes in Denver on a free-lance basis. Cerutty wanted disciples who could teach his running technique, not so much world-record holders. As I worked on this book, I would send copies of each chapter to Percy for his critical evaluation. He would write back giving a complete analysis of my thoughts, always ending his letters with the same message: "Your neural pattern philosophy will be the key to the world records of the future!"

In this chapter, I present my neural pattern philosophy, which complements Cerutty's Stotan philosophy. The athlete should know about conditioning neural patterns so he can make the change to Cerutty's five basic movements. Even more importantly, the athlete will be able to be in a 100% flow with his neural patterns. Herb Elliott had an undefeated career as a miler because he was always in harmony with his neural patterns. Herb's mind and body were balanced with Cerutty's Stotan training system. Elliott was never put into a hypnotic trance before a race.

A neural pattern is a habit pattern in the athlete's brain that is transferred to the right muscles in the body to produce a consecutive chain of motions called movement. Movement is running, jumping and throwing.

What Cerutty did when he taught me the five basic movements at Portsea was to develop a new neural pattern in my brain. This involved training the mind to carry different impulses away from the brain (efferent nerves) and those that send sensations to the brain (afferent nerves). If the athlete practices and concentrates on these natural movements regularly, these nerves will eventually carry new impulses to the muscles to replace the old neural patterns.

The cumulation of this learning was the creation of a new movement called a *major neural pattern.* The various steps practiced were the *minor neural patterns.*

When an athlete practiced galloping up a hill, one of Cerutty's five movements for natural running, he was conditioning a minor neural based on strengthening the lungs. When the athlete practiced it enough to flow the gallop with the other four movements, the technique would become the major neural pattern, and be second nature.

The Brain. When the athlete reconditions his mind with each one of the minor neural patterns, he will be flowing the parts of his major neural pattern together. This process takes time, patience and work. As the person practices the five basic movements, he will store the nerve impulses in his brain.

It is important that the coach correctly demonstrate the proper technique to an athlete so he can register the correct neural patterns in his brain. The eyes act as a camera to photograph the different motions (minor neural patterns). An athlete with a photographic mind can learn the five basic movements in just a couple of practice sessions. For the average person, it takes longer.

The area of the brain that is responsible for flowing the minor neurals and major neural patterns together is the cerebrum. The cerebrum, cerebellum and brain stem all work together to produce the five basic movements.

The athlete strengthens his major neural pattern

with *passive neural patterns* such as diet, weight lifting, gymnastics, hill running and surging on the spot. All of these parts of the neural pattern fit together in an unbreakable chain. To foolishly neglect any one of these important areas would result in a performance that is below the athlete's full potential.

The Neural Bond. This is a neural element that connects several minor and major neural patterns in their proper order or sequence. Athletes in two or more events like the decathlon and pentathlon connect many major neural patterns during the hours of a track meet.

Alberto Juantorena of Cuba had both of his major neural patterns bonded together in the 1976 Olympics when he won the 400 and 800 meters. The same is true of Emil Zatopek when he won the 5000 and 10,000 meters, and the marathon at the 1952 Olympics in Helsinki.

Forming the correct neural patterns is 80% of winning on the highest levels of competition. It is all mind over matter.

Before all of Elliott's races, he would go through the ritual of meditating on his neural patterns. Percy Cerutty hid Herb in a quiet place near the running track so spectators and reporters could not destroy his concentration for the race.

The Golden Harp. A major neural pattern with a rhythmic flow is like a great, golden harp. In the beginning, the child is capable of making beautiful music. But as time passes with age, the person's movements become dull like the harp strings that have not been tuned. Rather than try to retune the harp, the musician allows it to grow more out of tune so all sound loses its coherency. Cerutty's movements are an attempt to retune the runner's rhythmic vibrations or neural patterns so his full potential will not be wasted.

All athletes are like golden harps. They have to learn new neural patterns when the old ones become outdated or when a new technique is developed by

someone else in the world. In most cases, conditioning a new neural pattern like the five basic movements will free the athlete so that he can express his personality on the highest creative plane.

3

Five Basic Movements

I hold that the traditional movements accepted as good style in running are not good style," said Percy Cerutty.

This theory, like all of his others, was hererodox or opposed to accepted standards. He pointed out that heterodoxical theories are the only kind which can advance mankind. These type of theories are almost invariably rejected at first, then gradually gain acceptance. Many accepted ideas which are taken for granted are just waiting to be proven false. Percy cited the long-held theory that the earth was flat as the most profound example.

"Nature hates orthodoxy," Percy said. "Without variation, there is no evolution. Nature hates the even-beat, unvaried movements that we see today with the world's best runners."

Cerutty believed that athletics had reached a dead end, that there was no place for it to go if it clung to the orthodox way of movement. Hours of practicing using these movements could only, at best, cut a few seconds off of a runner's time.

The most obvious problem athletes have is that they don't properly use their lungs. The oxygen debt runners experience in races or vigorous training could be reduced with what Percy termed "full-lung aeration." The amount of oxygen that comes into the upper and lower lungs when fully filled is approximately 3500 cubic centimeters. In the orthodox method, the lungs only take in about 1500 cubic centimeters.

Percy's techniques of natural movement, which he taught me at Portsea and qualified me to carry on teaching throughout the world, were designed to get more oxygen into the upper lobes of the lungs, which would lead to more efficient and faster running. Percy told me that if an athlete were taught to utilize his lungs fully, he could cut huge margins off his best time. After a year with Cerutty, I had no doubt that the development of full-lung aeration could completely revolutionize the world of athletics. This may sound like a bold statement, but the evidence indicates it is true.

FULL-LUNG AERATION

Percy's theories about full-lung aeration were the direct result of personal experience.

"Because of my defective lungs when I contracted double pneumonia," he said, "I just had to learn to breathe deeper and completely fill my lungs. I found that running in the orthodox fashion limited my stride and prevented me from fully filling my lungs."

Percy worked on his own running movement, experimenting with different methods of running, in search of one that would more efficiently utilize his lungs.

"The runner cannot *suck* oxygen into his lungs," Percy said. "He has to take the pressure off the upper lobes of the lungs or they will never fill. The lungs are made up of tiny air sacs, not muscles. When the shoulders come up to shorten the muscles in the neck, this motion alone takes the pressure off the upper lobes so that oxygen can rush in naturally."

Lifting the shoulders allows more oxygen to rush into the lungs. This is the principle that runners need to understand and practice. The reason most runners are worn down in a race is simply because of a lack of oxygen to oxidize the glycogen that is fed to the working muscles.

Cerutty said that when the miler learns to gallop with full-lung aeration, he would be able to cut 5-10 seconds off of each lap.

Cerutty admired Emil Zatopek's "uninhibited" action, which helped win him four Olympic gold medals.

The chief means of filling the lungs, while lifting the shoulders, is to vary the arm movements. Emil Zatopek was the best example of this. He forced more oxygen into his lungs when other athletes were succumbing to oxygen debt and the build-up of lactic acid in their muscles.

Athletes work to avoid oxygen debt. They think that the more they train, the closer they can come to preventing, or at least delaying, its development in a race. It is true that the more one runs, the more he will be able to run with less oxygen need. But, as long as he is only filling one-third of his lungs, he can never hope to avoid oxygen debt and reach his true potential. Learning deep breathing is much more valuable than simply piling up miles in practice.

"It is not elaborate training schedules where the athlete runs 20 miles a day that will advance athletics," Percy said. "The athlete has to realize that walking is something the infant learns, and imitates, from his parents at a very early age. The child copies the poor examples that he sees in his parents and teachers, which is totally unnatural."

What Percy called the "zombie-like" way of movement is adopted by everyone. People believe it natural simply because everyone does it. It is wholly unnatural and greatly inhibits breathing.

"The breathing must be deep and slow," Percy said, "preferably every four or six strides. The carbon dioxide should be immediately exhaled. It is no good holding the carbon dioxide in the lungs when it has done its job."

Through experiments with himself and the athletes at Portsea, Percy devised the "five basic movements," which, when combined, served as the means of developing full-lung aeration.

THE FIVE BASIC MOVEMENTS

Children instinctively know how to fill their upper lobes, because they are so in tune with nature. Percy said that if we were left with just what nature had provided us, most of us couldn't survive. Elliott called the United States the most artificial country in this respect. As great as we think we are, if left with just what God provided, we are hopelessly crippled.

The orthodox movement we have adopted is symbolic of our neurotic, inhibited culture. The athlete who uses the zombie-like method lacks all the creativity and spontaneity that he was gifted with as a child. He conforms to society's norms without knowing what is really right or wrong.

Most runners know just three movements: walking, jogging and running. Percy's alternative involved five movements, each of which flowed into the next.

The stretch-up and walk. This sets the other movements in motion. As the runner begins to move, he naturally stretches upward, his arms reaching in the air above his head. This motion takes all the tension off of the muscles in the neck and back, and lets the runner feel loose all over. After stretching-up a couple of times, the runner should begin to walk, with his eyes looking down about 10 feet in front of him. His feet should be turned slightly inward.

The amble. The forearms should be thrown forward at shoulder length, almost parallel to the running surface, as the person frees his musculature while he starts to fill his lungs.

The amble starts the runner moving with a natural lift in his pelvis as he moves lightly over the ground with an effortless shuffle. His elbows should not be locked in position; they should be free and loose.

The amble is something children will naturally break into as they walk down the street. It is not quite a run but is gradually leading to one.

The trot. In the trot, the runner's arms come down from his shoulders and chest after the amble is done a couple of times. Then, the arms are pulled up and down to correspond with the breathing. The stride should be shorter than for both the canter and the gallop.

The canter. Like a horse, the runner should bound over the ground with an easy, relaxed shuffle. Cerutty often advocated this to break up the monotony of running many miles.

The important aspect of the canter is that the whole body should shift slightly to a dominant foreleg and hindleg style that is typical of all four-legged animals. Emil Zatopek had a natural gait in his running technique that was very similar to the free-form canter. The marathon runner will use a modified canter, a combination of the canter and the gallop, to conserve his strength and energy over the long race.

The gallop. This is the final and most crucial movement. Race horses gallop with a stride that is 20-30 feet long. The average human could easily gallop with a nine-foot stride.

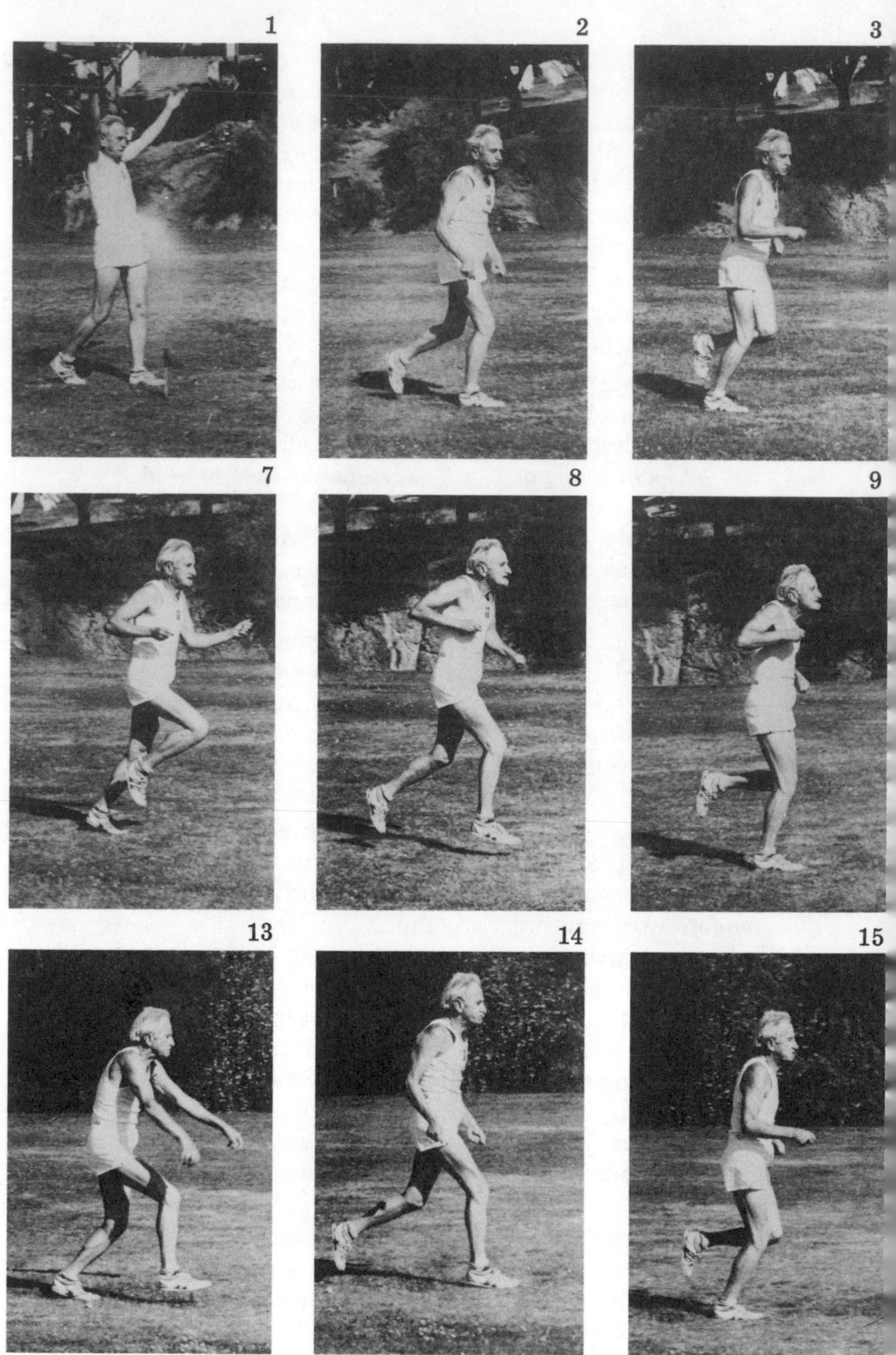

Percy Cerutty demonstrates the "amble." In the first two photos, he is stretching up and taking a step to move into the amble. In photos 3-7, he is inhaling oxygen in the upper lobes of his lungs. In photos 8-9, he holds air in his lungs. The carbon dioxide is expelled in photos 10-14. Photos 15-18 start the

process again with inhalation of oxygen. Note the position of the forearms as they come high in front of the chest to help the oxygen rush into the upper lobes of the lungs. Carbon dioxide is quickly expelled as the forearms are thrown downward.

The runner should change his arm movements abruptly as he brings his forearms up high into his chest, shortening the muscles in his neck. This takes the pressure off of the upper lobes of the lungs so that the athlete can fill his lungs with oxygen. Once the lungs are fully filled, the athlete should throw down his arms at his side to expel the carbon dioxide.

When the runner gallops, his stride length will vary with this inhaling and exhaling of oxygen and carbon dioxide. The outgoing stride, in which the athlete throws his forearm to his hind leg, should be 3-6 inches longer than the other stride, in which he fills his lungs.

The gallop should vary slightly depending on which event the person is training for. In the sprints, for instance, the runner's arms should be held lower than in long-distance running, because this elicits more strength from the upper body, which is crucial to sprinting.

When I was learning Cerutty's running technique, I found that the two terms a *puller* and a *galloper* were confusing until he showed me the difference. Percy said, "The puller uses the same arm actions like a trotter who runs with the even-beat, 'zombie-like' method of running. The gallop is a harder gait that calls for more strength and flexibility."

Adopting these five basic movements will not only improve oxygen consumption, it will also increase a runner's stride length. When Percy said that distance runners should develop a nine-foot stride, through the five basic movements, he wasn't speaking idly.

"During Herb Elliott's day," he said, "when I ran with the five basic movements, I could run with a nine-foot stride, which is much longer than most people of my size (5'7", 130 pounds) have. Everywhere I went, people were amazed by this stride. Now, at 80 years of age, I can only run with a seven-foot stride, which is still better than most of the 5000- and 10,000-meter runners. Only by using the five basic movements will the runner be able to run with a longer stride and completely fill his lungs with the same amount of energy that he uses when he runs in the orthodox, 'zombie-like' style of running."

After working with and teaching me his ideas on the five basic movements for a year at Portsea, Percy gave me a diploma allowing me to teach his techniques to others. When he came to the United States in 1974, I toured with him, teaching the five basic movements at clinics in California.

The basic idea is that the five basic movements should flow into one another, so that they carry the runner over the ground in one graceful movement.

I would teach it on five consecutive days. On Monday, I taught the proper stretch-up and walk, on Tuesday I taught the amble, on Wednesday the trot, on Thursday the canter, on Friday the gallop, and ending with a combination of all five movements flowing together into one, welding together the five links on the chain to natural movement.

Lengthening one's stride is essential to running. Percy lengthened his own stride, through the five basic movements, by more than 12 inches up to a full nine feet. He believed that anyone's stride could be lengthened by a foot or more without expending any extra energy. If this was done by the top runners, the world record for the 100-yard dash would be 8.0 and the record for the six-mile would be 24:00. (The current marks are 9.0 and 26:47.)

He points out, though, that once the new, lengthened stride is developed, it will demand more upper body strength, thus the need for weight training.

This idea seemed to predict bigger, stronger middle-distance runners such as John Walker and Alberto Juantorena.

Already Cerutty's ideas have begun to infiltrate the athletes of the future. Their impact probably won't be fully felt for many years to come.

There are several reasons why the theories of

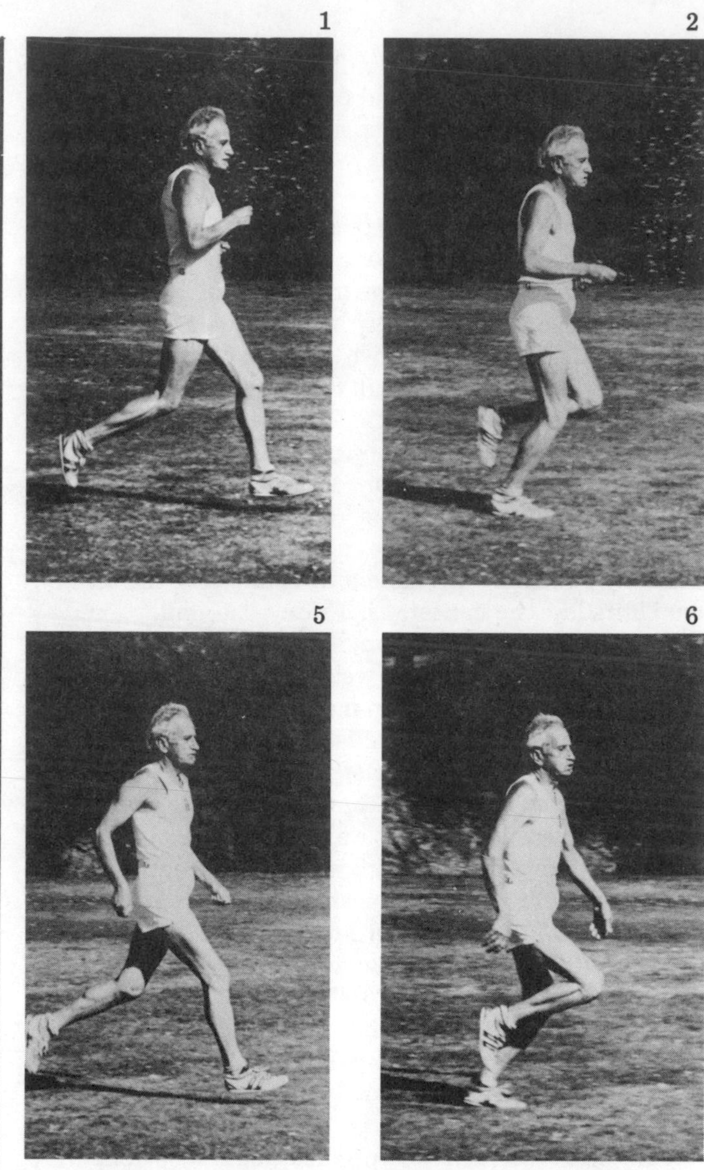

Percy Cerutty demonstrates a modified gallop which is used in middle and long distance events. In photos 1-2, he inhales oxygen into the upper lobes of the lungs. In photos 3-4, he holds the air in momentarily. Photos 5-6 show

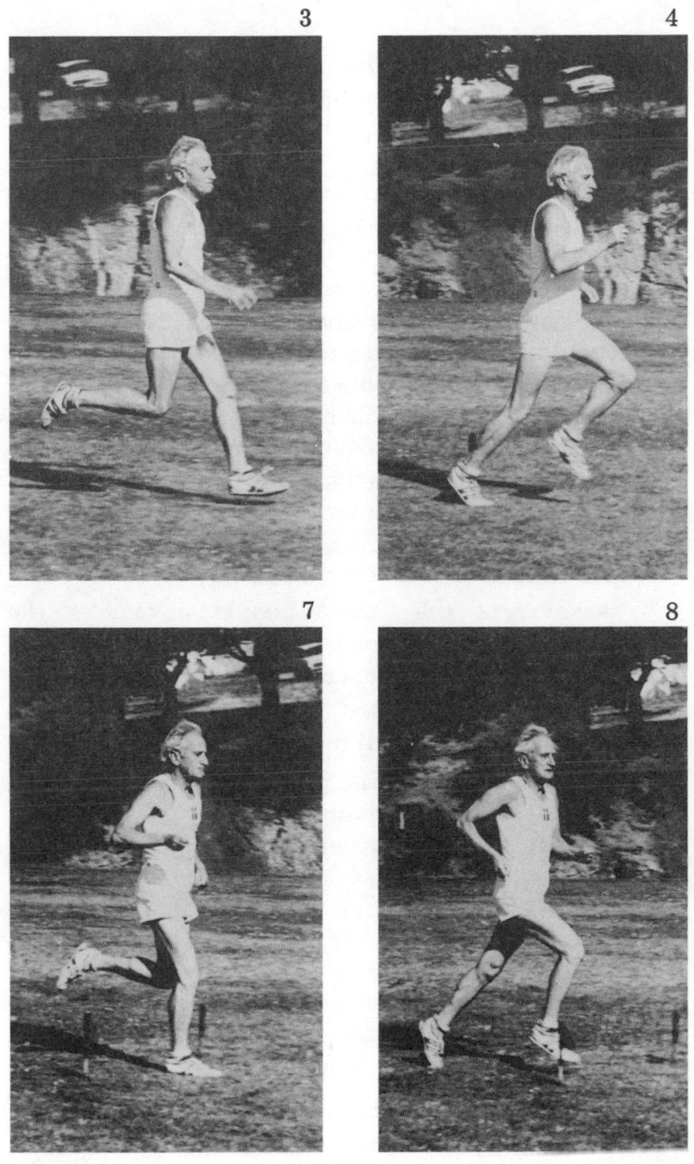

exhalation of carbon dioxide. The galloping movement starts again in photos 7-8. This sequence is a good example of two-hand downward thrust and spring-back.

full-lung aeration and the five basic movements have not immediately been adopted. The most obvious is simply that it differs from the accepted standard way of running.

"Man is deathly afraid to leave the artificial securities he has created for himself," Percy said. "This is why he is so slow to advance. New ideas aren't welcome. People are afraid of them. They're afraid to think for themselves and be original."

The unnatural movements that are seen throughout the world by top runners is largely caused by the fact that man has lost his basic instincts for survival by the way he eats, runs and exercises. This unnatural phenomenon is largely caused by the growth of technology. Modern man is ever dependent on machines, such as the automobile, to do things for him that he used to do for himself.

Because of this, most people have lost the instinctive, natural movement they were given at birth. The five basic movements were not some crazy radical idea from a gifted, eccentric coach they are a return to basic, natural movement.

Percy was called eccentric, even a genius, by some reporters. From my involvement with his camp, I can testify to his utter sincerity. So many coaches spout idealistic theories but aren't convincing because they don't practice them. Cerutty developed his theories not just through his athletes but through himself. He was his own guinea pig. He developed full-lung aeration, the five basic movements and a longer stride in himself. He didn't just talk about these ideas; he practiced them.

Once, before the high altitude 1968 Olympic Games, tests were made with the spirometer. The results showed the top athletes running with the orthodox method failed to even one-quarter fill their lungs. "It would have been far better for the runner to learn how to fill his lungs at sea level," Percy said, "than to train at high altitude with the zombie movements before they competed in the Games."

STYLE

The five basic movements are just part of an involved, complex theory of style that Percy designed for optimal running efficiency. He studies almost every aspect of human movement, looking for the most efficient means.

The stress in modern-day society on rigid posture is simply unnatural and cannot be reasonably kept up for any length of time. The usual result is an overcompensation and an extremely poor posture.

Once the runner has adopted the five basic movements and is running with a gallop, all of his joints should be in motion—including the elbow. One of the most common and energy-wasting problems runners display is shoulder sway. Shoulders should only move very minimally. The reason that they sway back and forth in most runners is that the arms are held too rigidly.

The arms should be carried low; they should never be at chest level. They should extend out and downward, with a definite "pull-back" as in swimming. The hands should open and close as if grabbing something. They should never be drawn back any farther than the runner's body. (They shouldn't be pulled back behind the runner's body, which is a common mistake most runners make.) One arm should be extended out farther than the other, just as one leg should be extended longer than the other.

The stride of one leg should be three inches longer than the stride of the other. When this style is in effect,the runner's trail leg won't rise higher than knee level. The feet should be pointed slightly inward. The very structure of the toes on the feet shows that the natural movement is to turn the feet inward while running.

"All natural running begins in the person's fingers and is transferred to the legs and feet," Percy said. "Dangling wrists or fingers create added tension. The fingers should be pinched together with a closed fist as the lungs are being filled. When the oxygen

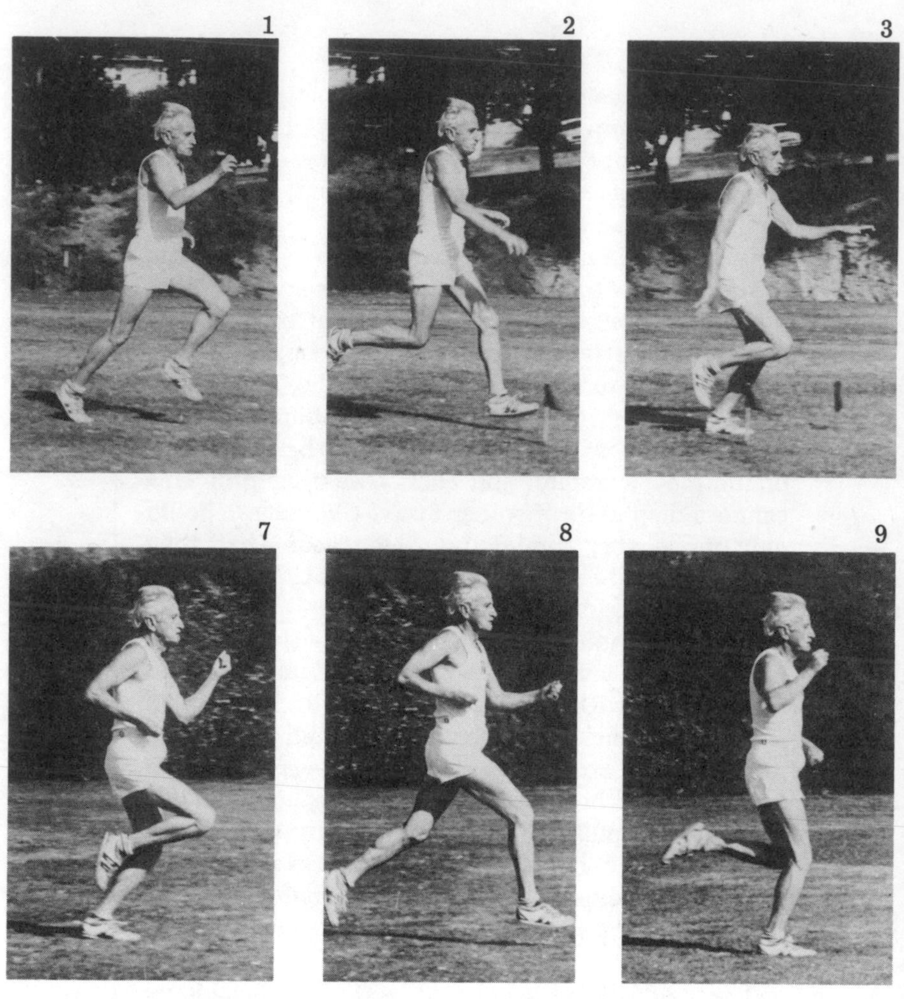

Percy Cerutty gallops in this series, with the lead forearm being throw down at the lead leg. In photos 1-3, Cerutty is exhaling the carbon dioxide from his lungs. In 4-7, he is inhaling oxygen into his upper lobes. Photos 8-9 show him holding the air in, and in photos 10-11 he is exhaling very

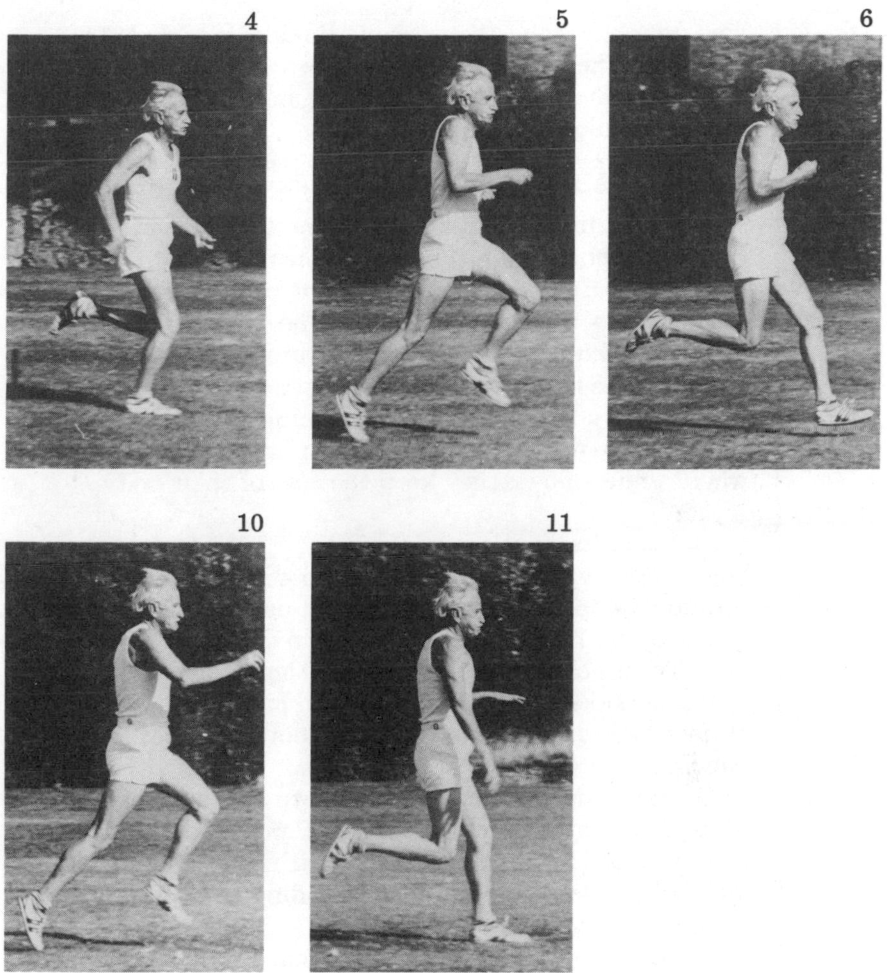

quickly as the forearms are being thrown down one after another. In analyzing the galloping movement, we can isolate the following factors: (1) a relaxed expression showing the absence of tension; (2) the eyes looking down at the ground; (3) proper head and body alignment; (4) a natural lift in the pelvis; (5) a low arm carriage, and (6) the knees and feet slightly in-turned.

has done its job, the carbon dioxide is exhaled rapidly as the hands are thrown downward. It is the downward motion of the arms and hands that forces the carbon dioxide out of the lungs.

"The hands should never move past the breast bone or sternum in the middle of the chest, nor should they move behind the seam on the side of the runner's shorts. All arm movement should be confined to the general area in front of, and below, the person's upper-body region. The elbows move about 3-5 inches on each side of the runner's trunk.

"The hands and wrists should never dangle or flap about. Many runners do this, thinking it will relax their body. Actually, it serves no purpose because when runners do it, they keep the rest of their body tense."

The runner must make sure that no part of his body is tense. While running, almost every muscle should be working—even the facial muscles.

The upper body should have only a slight forward lean. Too much lean causes awkward leg movement.

The outside edge of the foot should hit the running surface before the rest of the foot. Footfall should be almost noiseless.

"I teach the athletes at Portsea to run over the ground with an effortless shuffle," Percy said. "The runner skims over the ground with a slithering motion that does not make the pounding noise heard by a plodder who runs at one speed."

Olympic marathon champion Frank Shorter best exemplifies this nearly silent footfall.

All leg motions can be hampered if the athlete has a weak upper body. The only way to avoid tension in the legs is if the chest muscles are strengthened.

Cerutty believed that the runner should "lift his weight out of his pelvis." (The African distance runners seem to have the best grasp on this.) The pelvis should be tilted slightly upwards. This only can happen if the chest is relatively straight up and down. Those with a great protruding chest have difficulty moving their legs fast for a long distance.

Cerutty used Paavo Nurmi, the great runner from the 1920s, to illustrate the importance of low arm carriage.

"The knees and calves will naturally 'kiss' each other as one leg swings past the other during a gallop," Percy said. "A runner's legs will lift off the ground properly when the athlete learns to run correctly with a natural lift in his pelvis."

Percy believed that this lift alone could add as much as a foot to a person's stride, and advocated sit-ups to strengthen the mid-section.

One area that betrays the runner's tenseness is the

Emil Zatopek (right) never was restricted in his arm and head movements.

position of his head. The head should rest loosely on the person's shoulders. Cerutty found that if the neck and shoulders were relaxed, the rest of the body will be, too. If the head and neck are too tense, as most people's are, the shoulder lift that is needed for full-lung aeration is hampered.

When the body is properly aligned, with a slight forward lean, the runner should be able to turn his eyes downward so that he can see his knees coming up, without moving his head. In a normal running position, though, the eyes should be looking several yards ahead of the runner.

"The angle of lean for the body should be slightly forward with the head and eyes looking down about 10 feet in front of the runner," Percy said. "The neck and head should not be locked into any one position. The head should bob slightly as the forearms are thrown forward. The head should not tilt backwards at any time. Many close races have been lost by fractions of an inch because the runner carelessly let his head drop backwards, and disrupted his stride."

The head should easily be able to turn and look

behind without disrupting the runner's stride. This is usually a test of how properly relaxed the athlete is. Athletes who typified this were Zatopek and, more recently, Lasse Viren.

The chest and back should be relatively flat. This is the best position for allowing the shoulders to rise as they fill. The dead lift is the best exercise for training the shoulders for this upward motion.

Percy noticed Valeriy Brumel, 1964 Olympic high jump champion, had a good running technique because as he approached the bar, he brought his shoulders up high above his chest before he made the jump.

Several athletes have displayed parts of the natural movement Cerutty advocated. The athletes whose style differed from traditional movement have been the successful ones. Examples include Dick Fosbury, who invented a whole new way of high jumping (which has since become the accepted way) and won the Olympics with it, and such runners as Zatopek, Elliott, Arthur Newton, Rudolf Harbig, Gundar Haegg, Vladimir Kuts, Jack Lovelock, Paavo Nurmi and Kip Keino.

Cerutty believed that the problem of natural movement eventually would have to be met at its source—childhood.

"Most important is that the young children at the earliest age have to be taught the proper posture and to maintain the five basic movements so they fully fill their lungs. Breathing and posture: the most neglected things in running."

Since they aren't akin to accepted movements, the movements that Percy advocated had to be acquired through methods that weren't accepted. Running isn't enough. For the proper arm movements, the runner needs more upper body strength, hence weight lifting. But he also needs more than that.

The purpose of Percy's training was not to improve so much as it was to correct. The movement that so dominated athletics has simply run its course. It developed as far as it could and new breakthroughs in athletics depended not on training but on movement.

"A runner shouldn't come to me and ask *what* to run," Percy said. "He should ask *how* to run."

4

Natural Diet

Months of carefully planned, arduous physical training can be offset by a disregard for diet. Each time an athlete consumes a food substance with no nutritional properties, he is contributing to the deterioration of his system. The athlete can train every day, but if he is not digesting the proper foods, his training will not be giving him its full benefit. His system will have the extra burden of burning off the putrefaction derived from the dead foods as well as burning off the natural waste materials that are given off during exercise.

This extra work the body must undergo to oxidize the dead foods tears down the organism and negates much of the value of physical exertion. Eventually, if the body is fed on nothing but dead foods, it will lapse into a state of atrophy.

This situation occurred in Cerutty's life and was what led him on his search for the optimal diet. In 1938, the Postmaster General of Australia laid him off from work because he was too weak and run down to continue his job. When Percy consulted physicians, he was alarmed to learn that his body was in a state of atrophy, caused by an extreme mental and physical breakdown. He was told that unless the process was somehow reversed, he would be dead within a year.

When medication failed to remedy his problem, he turned to extensive research and experimentation. This led to the rebuilding of his body, cell by cell, in a completely natural way. For two years, he ate nothing but a pure diet of uncooked, organic foods. Day by day, he grew stronger. At first, it was an effort just to walk, but eventually he began to swim and run. In eight years, he would be the top ultra-marathoner in Australia.

He later very accurately referred to his recovery as a "rebirth." What Cerutty had done was create new, healthy cells in place of the old ones that were causing his problem. Eventually, he replaced every replaceable cell in his body, thus giving birth to a whole new healthy organism.

Of this rejuvenation, Percy said, "At first, I would go to the ocean and only have the energy to get wet to my knees. But in two years, I was doing 30-foot high dives off of the St. Kilda Pier."

Regardless of what amount of unnatural food you have ingested in your lifetime, the situation is to a large extent reversible. But each day you continue to eat this dead food, the reversing process becomes more lengthy and difficult.

The fact that unnatural foods have so saturated modern culture poses the most obvious problem. To this, Percy said, "To hell with social customs when your health is at stake."

Among the things that Cerutty believed harmful were animal fats (which putrify the intestinal tract), white flour and white sugar (which are carcinogenic, or cancer causing), salt, pepper and anything processed or refined.

The only adulteration he believed necessary was heating foods to rid them of possible poisonous sprays, microbes and bacteria. With today's large availability of natural foods, this is unnecessary.

Percy found that the ideal athletic diet was lacto-vegetarianism—which avoids meats but does not totally reject the products of animals, such as milk, eggs and cheese.

Protein can be acquired much more efficiently and safely than by consuming meat. Other sources include grains, nuts, eggs and cheese.

At Portsea, breakfast was always preceded by some form of physical activity, usually an hour of running or swimming. The habit of eating upon rising is an unnatural one, as the organism is not hungry until it has been up and moving around for a period of time. Percy believed that you should only eat when hungry. He always drew a distinction between appetite and hunger, believing most dietary problems to be a result of the widespread habit of eating when the body is not in demand of food.

The first meal of the day for Cerutty's athletes consisted of a bowl of raw, rolled oats, raisins, sultanas, nuts and fresh fruit. This was always eaten plain.

Lunch was generally a small meal, composed of fruits, cheese, soup or a vegetable, rice and celery salad.

For the evening meal, Cerutty's athletes would eat liver, chicken, fish and occasionally some mutton or beef. For the most part, they kept the animal proteins to a minimum.

Percy was strongly opposed to the long-standing idea that steak was the best pre-race meal. In fact, he called it among the worst possible, as it greatly impaired the digestive processes and tended to cause stomach irregularities.

The final formulation of his ideas was the result of lengthy trial and error and much study. He believed that these ideas were greatly responsible for the success of his athletes, almost as much as their development of proper movement and full-lung aeration.

FLUIDS

All natural fruit juices are more beneficial than tap water, soft drinks, whole or skimmed milk, alcohol, beer, tea and coffee. Milk is not an efficient nutrient and contains the danger of chemical poisoning. A person can obtain his daily requirement of calcium from other foods, such as potatoes and leafy vegetables.

Pure spring water is the best coolant for the system after physical exertion. It should be drunk lukewarm. Fruit juice is also good, especially after very long or difficult workouts.

Nature's best laxative is pure lemon juice with a teaspoon of honey and vinegar.

Fluids should never be consumed during the main course of a meal. They should be drunk at least a half-hour before the meal and then not again until 1 - 1-1/2 hours afterwards. The reasons for this are: (1) The fluids dilute the saliva and the digestive juices in the stomach, thus impairing the natural process of digestion; (2) The combination of food and liquid, particularly coffee and tea, leads to acidity of the heart; (3) The combination contributes to peptic ulcers.

A small glass of wine 15 minutes before the meal has been proven to be an aid to digestion. This is the only exception to the rule.

PROTEINS

Mild cheeses, grains, beans, nuts, eggs, fish, chicken and some vegetables provide a substantial source of protein for the human body. Beef is a very dangerous source, since the stock it comes from has very likely been fed with cancer-producing growth hormones. Countries in which vegetable consumption is high and meat consumption low also show a low incidence of cancer.

Two eggs can be substituted for a half-pound of beef, but should be eaten in moderation because they are high in cholesterol. It is much better to eat eggs that are produced on farms from chickens fed on grass and grains than ones from chickens at hatcheries, which have been fed on dangerous hormones.

Strong cheddar cheeses, cold cuts, lunch meats and pork are all very ineffective sources of protein which adversely affect digestion.

Frozen forms of animal protein are bad because

Cerutty praised wine as a drink which "aids in digestion." He recommended a small glass before meals.

the freezing process causes the food fibers to become too coarse for optimal digestion.

Protein consumption should always be minimal. There is no need for it to fluctuate with degrees of physical exertion. Tissue breakdown goes on at a constant rate and protein is a necessary builder of new tissue.

CARBOHYDRATES

Natural starches, sugars, vegetables and unbleached rice are highly recommended as sources of energy. Though they may seem to be high in calories, they are quickly oxidized by the system when the athlete is on a regular training program.

Potatoes are also a good source of carbohydrates. Baked potatoes in aluminum foil are recommended over boiled or mashed potatoes. French fries should be cooked naturally in safflower or some other vegetable oil.

Bread should be natural and wholemeal.

Processed breads, cereals and other carbohydrates are dead foods, serving no purpose whatsoever. They may taste good, but contribute to a deterioration of the system.

VEGETABLES AND FRUITS

All vegetables are best eaten raw. Heating them directly in hot water drains away their nutritional value. A more efficient way of heating them is by steaming them with water in a stainless steel basket.

Leafy green vegetables are very valuable because they provide a wide range of nutritional requirements and can supply the body's need for salt. They are also extremely low in calories.

Fruits should be eaten in season only. It is best to grow them yourself or to purchase them from a source which has grown them naturally. Like vegetables, they should always be washed carefully before consuming.

With all foods, careful chewing is extremely important. The breaking down of food in the mouth and the combining with saliva are integral parts of digestion. Gulping one's food greatly disrupts and hampers the digestion process, and can cause cramps and stitches during exercise.

Cerutty found that eating meals at the same time every day kept the body functioning consistently, without any irregularities. These designated times should be set so that the body responds with hunger symptoms shortly before each meal. Eating between meals disrupts the system.

If this schedule is adopted, specific quantity of food eaten at each meal is not important, as long as it is natural and the person is engaged in a regular program of physical exercise. Some of Cerutty's athletes would devour several huge bowls of oats, fruits and nuts in the morning.

Great amounts of water were often drunk by the athletes at Portsea two hours after meals. Whenever anything, liquid or solid, is ingested, there must follow a period of rest, in order to ensure proper digestion. Cerutty believed, however, that some physical exercise should always separate each meal.

For many people, eating is nothing more than an addiction, an opportunity to please their taste buds and corrode their system. Percy believed that we should eat to live, not live to eat.

He never took medication, because he felt that diet should serve as a form of preventive medicine.

"Some forms of cancer," he said, "and practically all colds and minor ailments can be cured with a diet of fresh fruit and uncooked vegetables. This is nature's best cure-all."

5

Strength Training

The most obvious problem with most running styles is a lack of strength, particularly upper body strength. Of all the several means of building strength that Cerutty advocated and which will be discussed in this chapter, the most crucial is weight lifting. Percy Cerutty was the first athletic coach in history to advocate that lifting heavy weights is an essential part of developing a distance runner. He was once vice-president of the Victorian Weight Lifting Association.

"Good running starts in the upper body and is then transferred to the legs," Percy said. "Strength is the main factor that will enable a person to reach his potential."

If the runner spends the conditioning period only building himself up aerobically, he is missing much of the point of Cerutty's theories. He should use this time to strengthen himself, thus making the basic movements easier, and giving himself a base for the race-practice period.

One reason many runners shy away from weight lifting is because they fear it will make them too top-heavy and muscle-bound, and ultimately will hurt their performance in distance running.

This is possibly true if they use the popular method of doing several sets of a half-dozen or more repetitions. This is the *extensive* method of weight lifting.

Most runners mistakenly use this, and it *does* tend

to add weight and bulky muscle. What they should be using is the *intensive* method of weight lifting. This involves working with the heaviest weight possible by doing short sets of three or four repetitions.

"There are two types of weight lifters—the weight trainer and the body builder," Percy said. "The weight trainer uses the intensive method to develop strength, whereas the body builder lifts weight with the extensive method to build up his body. The track and field athlete should practice with the intensive method so that he can build in *tensile strength* without experiencing any significant increase in body weight. With the extensive method, the body builder works with weights that are quite a bit lighter than his maximum lifting potential. He may do as many as 10-20 reps per set."

Tensile strength is what all runners need to develop, particularly distance runners. This improves an athlete's strength and power without adding extra weight. The extensive means of weight lifting just blows up the muscles in a person's body.

"The remarkable thing about the intensive method," Percy said, "is that the cells in the muscle fibers alter their composition and become a different color, instead of changing in size and growing bigger. This is characteristic of the extensive approach, in which the person puts a lot of unneeded bulk on his frame."

Greater strength without greater bulk requires that the number of repetitions not exceed five per set. Once this number is established for any exercise, the runner should never increase the amount of repetitions per set, only the weight being lifted.

"The runner's weight training should stress quality," Cerutty said. "It is far better for the athlete to lift the heaviest weight possible for him, in short sets of two or three, than to do a lot of repetitions. In distance running, the person will excel much faster by pulsing and surging at will with an uneven tempo, rather than covering the distance at an easy pace.

"Quicker reflexes can only be developed by gaining tensile strength through the lifting of heavy weights with the intensive method. It is ridiculous to believe the doctrine that athletes who are conditioned intensively with heavy weights are slowed down because they become muscle-bound and have their reflexes slowed. Herb Elliott and all of the runners who I have taught over the years and who set records around the world lifted heavy weights with the intensive method, and their reflexes weren't slowed at all. In fact, they were speeded up to a higher degree. Their inborn speed was enhanced even more."

Percy believed that many athletes, even some of the greatest champions, never reached their potential because they never developed the proper strength in their bodies. This was either because they didn't lift weights at all, or because they lifted them improperly.

"John Landy (former world mile record-holder) lifted weights with the extensive method," he said. "In my estimation, Landy's running career could have been far greater than it was had he conditioned himself intensively with heavy weights."

During the conditioning period of an athlete's program, which lasts six months, he should lift heavy weights three days a week, for about an hour or more each day. It is important at this period in training to combine aerobic, long-distance with weight training.

"In the race-practice period," Cerutty said, "which lasts three months, weight lifting should gradually taper off, so that by the last three or four weeks lifting will be done one day a week and then will cease entirely toward the end of the season.

THE BASIC LIFTS

Much as Percy devised the five basic movements to develop full-lung aeration, he had five basic lifting exercises for developing tensile strength. They were: (1) one-arm swing; (2) cheat curl; (3) bench press; (4) dead lift and (5) sit-ups.

The arm swing with dumbbells. (Cerutty preferred heavier weights than this athlete is using.)

One-arm swing. This lift is not only beneficial as a warm-up for the other exercises, but is also extremely valuable in building a neural pattern in the athlete's brain to enable him to lift his center of gravity out of his pelvis and be in perfect balance when he runs with the five basic movements.

In this exercise, the runner should work with a heavy dumbbell, approximately 1/3-1/2 of his body weight. The dumbell should be held firmly in one hand and then swung in an arc through the middle of the legs and over the head. The swinging arm should be completely straight. Be sure that the feet are planted directly beneath the shoulders. The arm that is not swinging should be extended to aid in balancing the athlete.

The proper breathing pattern is essential in this move. The athlete should fill his lungs with oxygen as the dumbbell is being lifted from the ground. As the weight is lowered, the lifter should exhale.

This move develops the athlete's upper body and breathing simultaneously, so it is crucial that the breathing be done properly.

Several swings should be done with one arm and then the weight should be shifted to the other one.

The starting (left) and finishing positions in the curl, using an underhand grip.

Since this is a swing and not an actual *lift*, the number of repetitions with one arm doesn't have to be limited to five and may, in fact, exceed 20. This move should always be the first one in a weight lifting workout since it leads into the other four.

When Percy toured the world with his athletes, he always brought along a 50-pound dumbbell (38% of his body weight) so he could practice this regularly.

Cheat curl. This lift is just what the name implies. The athlete bends the lower part of his back to help him curl a weight that is as much as three-quarters of his body weight. This lift is important in strengthening the muscles in the arms that are crucial in the five basic movements (supinators, pronators, biceps and triceps). This added strength allows the runner stronger and more varied arm movements, which leads to full-lung aeration and faster running.

This can be done with either an underhand or overhand grip, though the underhand grip is preferable. Some athletes alternate grips to develop different muscles.

Repetitions per set should be limited to five, with no more than two or three sets. At first, three-quarters of one's body weight might prove to be too difficult, but the athlete can build to this. Several of

Cerutty's athletes were able to do it with their full body weight.

Bench press. For upper body strength, the bench press is the best lift. It is especially good for developing the strength needed for the proper arm extension. It is also excellent for improving reflexes. Boxers do this to develop punching speed.

The athlete should lie on his back, flat against a bench, and press the barbell overhead until his arms are fully extended in the air over his chest. As he pushes the weight from his chest, the lifter should inhale oxygen into his lungs. When the weight is slowly lowered, the person should exhale.

This exercise should be done with the athlete's full body weight, and each set should be limited to two or three repetitions. Ideally, three sets of this should be done in the course of a weight workout.

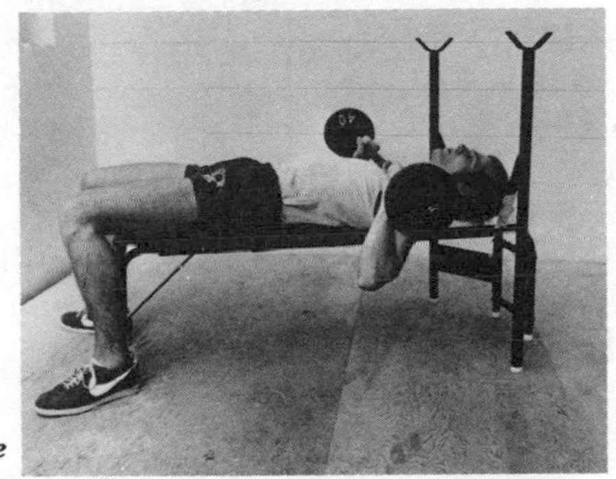

Two stages of the bench press, used to gain strength in the upper body.

Again, weight will vary with the individual. Some athletes at Portsea did this lift with 1-1/2 times their full body weight. Percy said that generally the runner should be able to curl three-fourths of his body weight and press or jerk his full body weight. This applies differently to women and to people of unusual builds.

Dead lift. The dead lift is the exercise for leg development, although it also strengthens the upper body and the back.

The athlete begins this lift by firmly planting both of his feet under the bar, directly below the shoulders. He should be lifting twice his body weight in this move. A reverse grip should be used, in which one hand wraps over the bar while the other wraps under it. The back should be bent at a 45-degree angle to the horizontal while the head is facing forward. The lifter should then bend his knees and lower his body almost to a sitting position. Good lifting posture is essential with this exercise. The runner can suffer from groin strain if he pulls the heavy weight off the ground with his back or stomach muscles.

When the athlete is in this crouching position, he should fill his lungs and then simply stand up, using his legs to lift the weight from the floor. He should stand to a full upright position, then expel the carbon dioxide from his lungs.

Once the athlete is in an erect position, he should lift his shoulders in a shrugging motion several times before letting the weight down. This additional motion is extremely valuable for exercising the muscles in the chest where the upper lobes of the lungs are located. This will aid the runner in filling his lungs and running more effectively with the five basic movements.

The dead lift greatly develops the thighs without making them bulky.

"I'm vitally opposed to over-developed thighs that are abnormally strengthened with the extensive method of weight lifting," Percy said. "Bulk strength in the thighs will slow the runner down considerably when he starts to run long distances. This is the main reason that most sprinters never make good milers or long-distance runners. Their thighs are too big. All athletes need tensile strength in their legs. The dead lift is more natural for developing muscles in the thigh than doing deep knee bends, half squats or toe raisers using weighted shoes or a leg press machine."

The dead lift is especially valuable for the jumpers, and they should do more of it than the long-distance runners, since they need more tensile strength in the thighs.

Sit-ups. This is the ideal exercise to end a weight training session. It is not actually a weight lifting exercise, but is the best means of strengthening the abdominal muscles, which are among the most neglected muscles in track and field athletes.

"Most all runners neglect to develop abdominal strength," Percy said, "and because of it they lack the leg power they should have when their legs are being lifted by the abdominal muscles."

Hurdlers need this exercise more than any other athlete, although all athletes should do them.

Cerutty oversees the sit-ups of athletes at Portsea. (Herb Elliott is at far right.)

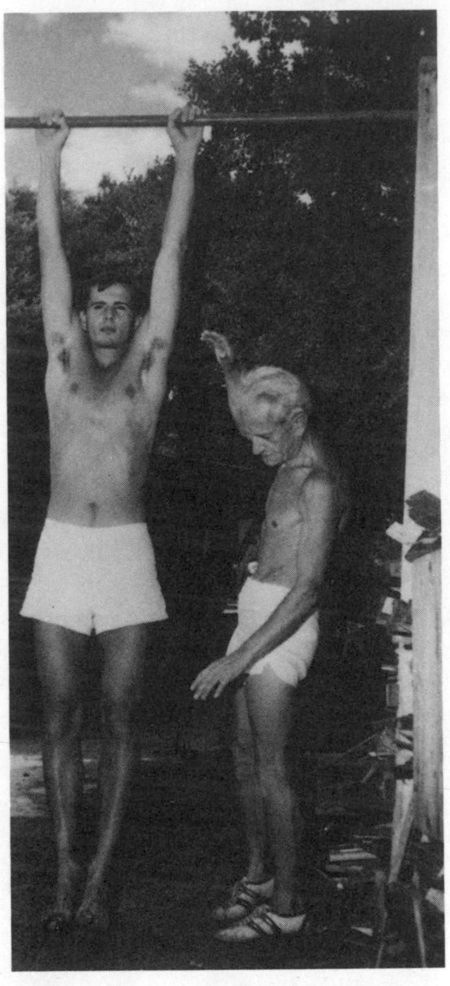

Hanging from a horizontal bar prevents muscles from shortening with weight lifting and hard running.

Most people who do sit-ups do them very inefficiently, totalling large amounts without any significant resistance. Just as with weight exercise, these should be done intensively rather than extensively. The most common way, with the hands clasped behind the head and the knees bent, is very inefficient.

Sit-ups should be done on an incline board with a weight held behind the head. This should start out as five pounds and steadily increase. As the sit-ups become easier, the athlete should not try to do more; he should increase the weight. This increase should be gradual. Many athletes at Porsea did these with weights of 25 pounds and more.

A good number of sit-ups is 20 or 25. During the conditioning period, three sets of these should be done in a day with 10, 20 and 25 pounds.

Cooling down. After these five exercises have been completed, the athlete should hang limp on a horizontal bar for approximately three minutes to relax the muscles in his body and prevent shortening of the muscle fibers.

There are a number of other exercises Cerutty recommended for building strength. Running up hills, particularly sand hills such as the ones at Portsea, was one. This develops the upper body movements and the thighs.

"Other than dead lifting a very heavy weight, I strongly recommend running up steep hills," Percy said.

Most runners bend their elbows with a high arc on a hill. This defeats the purpose of hill training by encouraging an awkward running style and wasting energy. When an athlete reaches a hill, he should *lower* his arms and thrust them in a low arc. The lower the arms are carried, the faster he can climb the hill.

Another error runners make on hills is bringing their knees up too high. This is a totally wasteful movement. If the arms are carried low, this is automatically discouraged.

Developing the low arm position on hills is extremely beneficial when the runner comes to a track. Running with the proper movements and running *fast* will seem easier than if all training had been on the flat.

Hills should be run intensively, with several repetitions. The number of repetitions is based on the grade of the hill, of course. At Portsea, where the main hill was 80 feet of sand, some runners had trouble running up it once with full power. The hill should be grade of at least 1-2.

When running downhill, most runners have the tendency to come down very hard with each step. This is inefficient and wastes energy. It causes the runner to come downhill too fast, and leaves him tired on the flat. This is especially harmful when the downhill section is followed by another uphill climb, because the runner will have little energy for it.

The proper downhill running technique involves keeping the body straight with the strength of the abdominal muscles. Athletes who run a lot of cross-country should work on strengthening these.

The runner should always be in total control of himself when he is running downhill so he won't fall and injure his knees. He should rest shortly while the momentum carries him down the hill. This will conserve his valuable energy and improve his surging power for a race.

A good hill workout involves hard uphill running, then an easy controlled descent before starting uphill again.

Besides hill training, gymnastics is an activity highly recommended for all athletes. This develops tensile strength throughout the body, aids agility and breaks up the sometimes boring regularity of training for a specific event. Particularly in the conditioning period, gymnastics should be included, on the non-weight lifting days.

"On the days of the training week that the athlete is not doing the five basic lifts, he should do gymnastics work," Cerutty said, "to develop his strength and coordination. The gymnastics work should include chin-ups, rope climbing using only the arms, working on the parallel bars, the vaulting horse, the Roman rings and jumping on the trampoline. The trampoline and vaulting horse are especially valuable for athletes in the jumping events."

The idea of breaking up the routine of running (or whatever the athlete's event is) with a supplemental exercise is crucial. It hardly matters what the exer-

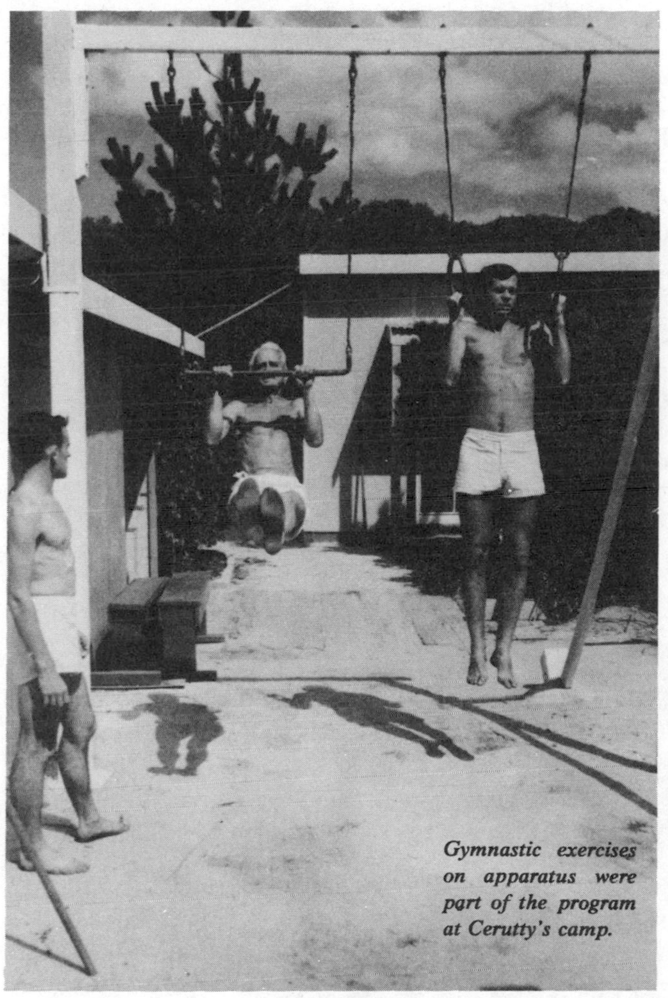

Gymnastic exercises on apparatus were part of the program at Cerutty's camp.

cise is as long as it doesn't alter the neural patterns. Cerutty's athletes did such diverse things as mountain climbing, swimming, skiing, boxing and surfing. Herb Elliott played the piano to improve his tempo and rhythm for running.

This is not to say that the athlete shouldn't individually work on the specific areas of his sport that need improving, just that there should be some work that is directly related to an athlete's event.

"In addition to the five basic lifts, gymnastics and other exercise, the athlete should do some extra lifts and training, according to his own particular needs," Cerutty said. "He can do leg lifts with a weight on his feet while he is lying prostrate, rowing motions with a dumbbell 1/3-1/2 his body weight, push-ups on his fingertips and the prone press. The weightmen (shot putters and discus throwers) will add additional power lifting to the five basic lifts. These should include the clean and jerk, half squat and military press."

Supplementary strengthening can come from manual labor if one's work requires it. Many of the athletes at Portsea earned their keep by doing work around the camp.

Albert Thomas was another of the Cerutty-trained world record-holders. He was fastest at two and three miles.

Of course there must be a limit to one's supplementary training some athletes do too much. Most of it should be balanced with running during the six-month conditioning period.

"If you want to be a runner, then you must mostly run," Percy said.

Running and strength building for the athlete's main event should take priority, and other activities should serve the purpose of keeping this training from becoming monotonous. At Portsea, the runners swam regularly after their afternoon workout.

Many athletes have injured themselves in sports that were not their speciality and sometimes were knocked out of serious competition. So, involvement in extra activities should be concentrated in the six-month conditioning period, and though it is essential to break the tension of the main competitive period, it should then be limited to safe sports such as swimming, tennis and golf.

Besides the risk of injury, introducing other activities in the crucial racing season can throw off the athlete's timing, which should be tapering down with strict quality work.

The most important point of all strength building work is that it must be a difficult exertion to have benefit. It must be vigorous. It has little value for a track and field athlete (or long-distance runner) if it doesn't require a hard effort. It must involve strong resistance, such as the heavy weight of a barbell or the sand on a hill. Any resistance exercise has value (such as running with leg weights) as long as the athlete does it intensively with the purpose of building tensile strength.

"My advice to all athletes," Percy said, "is that they should lift the heaviest weights and run up the steepest hills, particularly in the conditioning period, by using the intensive method of building strength. This will help athletes in every event."

The reason that it is important to do this in the conditioning period is because the runner will be able to handle the extra workload when he starts racing. With the added strength, the basic movements become easier and the runner can breathe more easily so by the start of the race-practice period, his oxygen consumption is in excellent shape and he is able to handle faster work and track racing.

Cerutty shows the importance of a flat back, which influences one's running posture.

Most athletes don't make the transition to fast running very effectively because their lungs haven't been properly developed. They've spent the conditioning period plodding through miles of running with improper movement. When fast running is introduced to the program, they spend the whole competitive period struggling with oxygen debt, because their lungs are simply not equipped to handle the faster running.

"It is physical strength that breeds real confidence in the athlete's personality," Percy says, "so that he can express himself in his event. By lifting heavy weights, the runner can pull on his strength to win close races as Elliott did many times. The stronger that athlete develops himself by lifting heavy weights to strengthen his upper body, the better he will perform overall. Only the fit are fearless!"

II

THE RUNNING EVENTS

Sprinting and Hurdling

The sprints and hurdles were not events with which Cerutty was a specialist. However, he did study them extensively, and trained Betty Cuthbert along with many other sprinters at Portsea. He worked with the 1960 Olympic 100-meter champion Armin Hary when Elliott was competing in Sweden.

Sprinters are similar to distance runners in that they are uneconomical in their running movement. They train very inefficiently and never learn to use their lungs properly.

Percy advocated a modified version of the gallop for sprinting, with the arms held low, reaching out and down in a low swinging arc. One stride should be longer than the other.

The orthodox style, Percy believed, showed a complete lack of relaxation; it was paradoxical and self-defeating. The athlete appeared to be straining from the beginning, but actually he was only causing himself to run slower by keeping his body so tense. He ran unbalanced and uneconomically.

The sprinter should be especially concerned with lengthening his stride. This is one of the most important concepts for improvement in sprinting. If he runs with the proper arm and leg movements, the sprinter should be able to lengthen it by as much as a foot. It is harder for the sprinter to do this than the distance runner because his race is so short and so fast, but it is something that must be developed. Percy found that this could improve the sprinter by more than a full second at 100 yards.

Sprinting should be a built-in neural pattern in the athlete's brain. He should be born with it. A top sprinter should have the urge to sprint when just walking down the street. He shouldn't just have it when he's on a track.

Valeriy Borzov, winner of the 1972 Olympic 100- and 200, is a good example of this. "Sometimes, I can't even walk and I change automatically to a running stride," he said, "before I realize that I am in no hurry."

This natural idea of running is not encouraged by most training programs, which are so separated from daily living that the athlete tries to forget it, to block it out of his daily activities. He doesn't enjoy it because he convinces himself it has to be unpleasant to be beneficial.

Cerutty also disagreed with the basic hurdling movement: that the arm opposite the lead leg should be extended over the hurdle. He believed that if the lead leg and arm were both on the same side, the runner could move faster over the hurdles.

His ideas on breathing were opposed to the ideas of his contemporaries, but have since been adopted by several top sprinters and hurdlers.

The 100-yard dash runner should start the race with his lungs filled, and then take just three inhalations during the race.

The hurdler should inhale over the hurdles and exhale between them.

"Rod Milburn (1972 110-meter Olympic champion) is the only hurdler I have ever seen who could breathe properly in a race," Cerutty said.

Since his own involvement was in distance running and his camp attracted mostly racers of a half-mile or more, Percy never had the opportunity to work with sprinters and hurdlers as much as he wanted. But he considered these to be areas most in need of development.

TRAINING

Cerutty divided training for every event into three

Cerutty advised Olympic 100-meter champion Armin Hary on his running style.

phases: the conditioning, race-practice and competition periods. The conditioning period is strictly non-competitive, lasts for six months and is designed to build a strength and endurance base so that the athlete is better able to handle the more intense work in the race-practice period. The race-practice period generally lasts for three months. The competition period lasts the remaining three months of the year.

Sprinting. For sprinters (and hurdlers) distance

running is important to develop a base of stamina and endurance. Cerutty's special prescription for sprinters in the off-season is simply to stay in shape, mostly through sports other than running. Basketball, tennis, swimming and soccer are all ideal.

There should be some distance running every day —2-5 miles—and several sessions of wind sprints. The athlete should lift heavy weights at least twice a week, preferably three times. This should be intensive lifting which includes cheat curls, one-arm swing, bench press and dead lift.

The conditioning period is also when the runner should work on lengthening his stride. It is very helpful to watch films to assess your stride. One stride should be longer than the other, as in galloping.

The arm movement should be out and down, and there should be no shoulder sway. If the shoulders are held steady, the arms can propel the runner and build his momentum. This is why upper-body development is so important.

Arm movement is the basis for a longer stride and should be developed during the conditioning period. The sprinter needs this base before doing specific sprint workouts. He should try to develop his stride and his speed simultaneously, as the two go together for a fast race.

During the race-practice period, training should stress quality rather than quantity. Weight training should be cut to twice a week, and then tapered, to once a week in the competitive period.

All non-track work should vary proportionately to the length of the racing distance. A 220 sprinter, for instance, should do more distance training and weight work than a 100-yard dash runner.

One of the major problems with sprinters is that they take too long to accelerate. This can be remedied with proper training. Percy called the quick, immediate starting movement the "surge." This can be acquired by making practically all training at maximum effort (with the exception of one easy distance run per week). One exercise Percy advocated for developing this movement was running in place, on grass, as fast as possible for several seconds.

The athlete should only go to the track twice a week during this period, to practice segment running, running the race in thirds. He should work up to a gallop for the full distance of the race by adding the segments together and doing an occasional over-distance sprint so that in the racing situation the sprinter can go the full distance at the same intensity for each segment.

Starting should be practiced on the two track days, but only minimally. Part of practicing starts is practicing proper breathing. The sprinter should fill his lungs immediately before the start and begin expelling carbon dioxide with the first stride. This is what Cerutty taught Armin Hary, winner of the 1960 Olympic 100-meter race.

"Releasing the tension in the epiglottis gives the sprinter a great boost at the start," said Percy. "The boost is similar to a pressure-filled bottle that shoots its cork."

The ideal start is a product of this expelling of carbon dioxide and developing dynamic movement.

The sprinter should practice what Cerutty called "surging," which is starting with the lungs full of oxygen and then running the first one-third segment.

As the race-practice period evolves, training should decrease in volume and increase in intensity. Toward the end, when the sprinter has regular important races, he should limit it to wind sprints and a few starts.

A sample sprinter's week of workouts during the race-practice period:

Monday—starts, segment running, wind sprints.
Tuesday—weight lifting, stretching.
Wednesday—wind sprints on grass, varied pace running.
Thursday—cross-country run, four miles.
Friday—weight lifting, gymnastics.
Saturday—starts, segment running, wind sprints.
Sunday—Rest.

Hurdles. Training for the hurdles is very similar to training for the sprints, with two main differences. The hurdler should do more supplementary exercise such as weight lifting, calisthenics, gymanstics and hill running, and obviously he should jump hurdles in practice, learning his steps between hurdles so that they come naturally.

The one area the hurdler has to work on the most is running with his lead arm and leg extended simultaneously from the same side. Since this is directly opposed to the orthodox way of hurdling, it will be difficult at first, but once it is learned, it will seem more natural and easier than the orthodox style. It will also allow the runner greater speed over each hurdle. One reason is that it won't let him go too high in the air between hurdles. Many hurdlers have great speed and have their steps down precisely, but are slowed by jumping too high over the hurdles.

Additional exercises the hurdler should implement into his program are sit-ups on an incline board, or other abdominal strengthening exercises, and general flexibility work such as gymnastics.

Developing strength is equally important for the hurdler and for the sprinter.

"In hurdling," Percy said, "It is essential that the runner develop the proper *power* and *strength* to have a good technique. He must do intensive weight lifting to develop his accelerating power.

A sample week early in the hurdler's race practice period:

Monday—segment running with hurdles, wind sprints.
Tuesday—weight lifting, gymnastics, sit-ups.
Wednesday—cross-country run, five miles.
Thursday—wind sprints on grass, varied running, sit-ups.
Friday—weight lifting, gymnastics.
Saturday—segment running with hurdles, wind sprints, sit-ups.
Sunday—rest.

RACING

Starting. Obviously, the start is a crucial part of a

sprint race. For some sprinters, it is their primary strength.

Cerutty had little against the orthodox starting position but felt that runners didn't use it properly. Most runners go through an elaborate procedure to start fast, then start slow. Usually, runners are slowed getting to a full upright position. This is why some sprinters recently have reverted to a standing start. But if used properly, Cerutty believed the block start to be superior.

The knee of the back foot should be in a position near the front foot. There should be a slight upward line from the rear to the shoulders. The sprinter's eyes should be aimed at an imaginary point on the track approximately where the rear foot will land in its first stride. He should keep his attention focused on this spot until the gun sounds.

One of the most common errors of sprinters is that they are too tense in the starting blocks and look down the track as they are waiting for the gun. This puts stress on the neck, shoulders and back, and leads to a slow start.

To charge out of the blocks like the runner should, he must be totally relaxed. As he looks at the spot on the track, his chin should drop limp. Percy equated

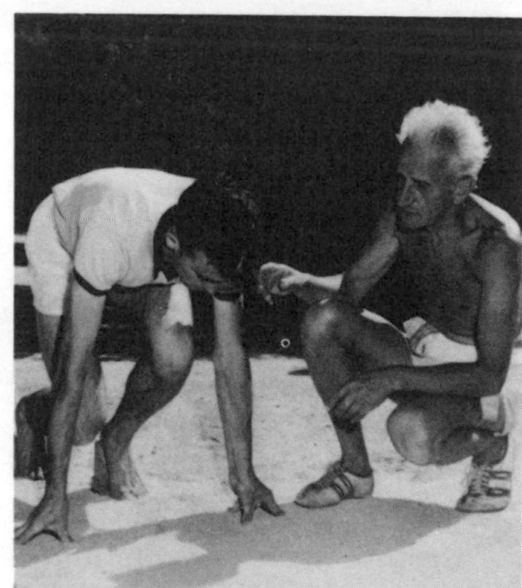

Cerutty teaches a sprinter the proper technique of coming out of the blocks.

the sprinter just before the gun is fired with a person who is sound asleep at night who jumps out of bed when he hears a fire engine outside, thinking his house is on fire. This is how the sprinter should react to the report of the starter's gun.

With the command "on your mark," the sprinter should instinctively begin to slowly fill his lungs with oxygen. This should be slow and steady, inaudible to the other competitors. Then, when the starter gives the "set" command, the lungs should be completely full so that the runner has to hold it for a second. When the gun fires, the runner explodes from the blocks. He should be out of his crouch in a full upright position by 30-40 yards. The hurdler should rise to this position slightly earlier.

Sprinting. When the race comes, the runner should put together the segments he has been running in practice.

The neural patterns for each third of the race should have been developed thoroughly in practice. The longer the race, the less the runner's intensity on the sprinter's part. But when the three segments are put together, the sprinter can capture the intensity for the full distance.

"Sprinters have to concentrate completely on their race because it is so short," Cerutty said, "but at the same time they can't be tense. It has to be relaxed concentration."

Proper sprinting should resemble the gallop, only the arms should be carried lower. Most sprinters are literally off-balance during races, and a major reason is because their arms are pumping completely recklessly. "Desperately," Percy said.

Keeping the arms in this low position not only keeps the runner in balance it also allows him the proper efficient breathing technique. A runner should only take one breath every 33-1/3 yards. Percy cited Bob Hayes, 1964 Olympic 100-meter gold medalist, as the one person who could do this best.

Hurdling. The only difference in sprinters and hurdlers is the series of barriers the hurdlers must jump over. But this is a tremendous difference.

The hurdler needs more strength and more dexterity than the sprinter. Top hurdlers have an amazing sense of balance. Ideally, the hurdler's legs should just clear the hurdles. "They should be able to skim a nickel off the top of the hurdle," Percy would say.

Building proper momentum between hurdles is crucial, and if the runner either clears the hurdle by too much, or particularly if he hits it, he will be unable to build this momentum. He will be wasting the time between hurdles trying to regain his stride.

When the hurdler has developed the Cerutty technique of having the same lead arm and lead leg, his trail leg will naturally recoil much faster than in the orthodox fashion, and this allows him to regain a quicker and more natural contact with the running surface.

In a perfect hurdle race, Percy believed that the runner should be running so naturally that he doesn't even realize he's jumping over hurdles.

7

400 and 800 Meters

At one time, the 440 was considered too long to be a sprint. Now, with runners like Mike Boit and Alberto Juantorena, the 880 is becoming a virtual sprint.

Training for these two races is similar to training for the sprints, in that the athlete should practice running segments of the race in practice.

Said Percy Cerutty of the 440, "By surging over the various sections of the quarter-mile at will, the sprinter will accomplish two things: (1) learn to move at the required speeds over his competitive distance that will instinctively be delivered in a race; (2) the athlete will be able to hold these hard efforts of long speed during the race so that he will not come up short in the quarter-mile by experiencing undue oxygen debt."

Traditionally, the 880 is grouped with the middle-distance races, and the top half-milers are actually mile specialists. But Percy believed that it should be grouped with the 440, and in fact he lectured on this at Portsea. Alberto Juantorena of Cuba is the runner who has proven that the two go together. He won both of them at the 1976 Olympics, setting a world record in the 800 meters.

"The quarter-mile and the half-mile require many of the same strengths," Percy said.

World-class 800 runner Mike Boit said, "The fact that Ralph Doubell could tie the world record for 800 meters at Mexico City proves that the 800 is not an aerobic event, but is an anaerobic event and should be grouped with the 400."

In fact, the 440 is about one-fourth aerobic, the 880 close to one-third aerobic and the mile approximately one-half aerobic.

Boit also said, "You have to think of the 800 as a sprint."

THE QUARTER-MILE

Most quarter-milers do not develop the proper neural pattern for running their event and thus find themselves struggling in the final fourth of the race. This neural pattern should be built by running 110, 220 and 330 segments, and an occasional set of 660-yard runs. Many runners neglect these over-distance intervals.

Once this neural pattern is developed and the proper movements are used, the sprinter should be able to maintain the speed he displays in a 100-yard dash over a full 440.

The conditioning period. In the conditioning period, the quarter-miler should do a lot of varied-pace cross-country running to develop cardiovascular strength. Many runners feel they don't need this, but they are usually the ones who can't maintain their sprint and become tied up with oxygen debt.

The quarter-miler should average between 20-40 miles per week. This should increase proportionately to the six-month conditioning period. Initially, this mileage should be achieved through three-mile cross-country runs at varied paces. But by the end of the conditioning period, the athlete should be able to run six miles in less than 30 minutes.

Three days each week, the 440 runner should spend at least an hour lifting heavy weights with the basic lifts. His lifting workout should be essentially the same as for the sprinter and hurdler, but with greater intensity. Once a week, the quarter-miler should do an hour of gymnastics.

No track training should occur in the conditioning

period. There should be some sprinting, but only in the course of a varied pace cross-country run or in sand hill training. There should be one long run per month, of 8-15 miles.

A sample week in the conditioning period follows:

Mornings

Cross-country running of 2-10 miles five days per week at a varied, but increasingly fast pace.

Afternoons

Monday: An hour of intensive weight lifting with the basic lifts.
Hang limp on the horizontal bar for two minutes.
Run on the spot for 10-15 minutes.

Tuesday: An hour of gymnastics.
Two miles at a varied pace.
Run in place for 5-10 minutes.

Wednesday: An hour of intensive weight lifting.
Two miles at a varied pace.
Run in place for 10-15 minutes.

Thursday: 30-45 minutes of surging up a hill with a grade of 1-2.
Run two miles at a varied pace.
Run in place for 10-15 minutes.

Friday: An hour of intensive weight lifting.
Hang limp on the horizontal bar for two minutes.
Run in place for five minutes in 30-second intervals

Saturday: Run six miles at a varied pace.

Sunday: Rest.

Race-practice period. Speed work becomes the major form of training once the race-practice period is underway. This should be done on the golf course, a park or other grass surface. Running should be at a varied pace, as is the conditioning period, but at a considerably faster overall rate. These runs should be largely anaerobic, as opposed to the aerobic nature of the conditioning-period runs. The runner should be thinking of the segments of his race as he surges over approximate 110, 220, 330 and 660 segments. If the athlete is able to keep up this varied-pace running for much more than an hour, then his overall pace is too easy.

Like the shorter distance sprinter, the 440 runner

should do some workouts in which he practices running thirds of his race, approximately 150 yards.

The quarter-miler should learn to run all-out over 150-yard segments, in practice, building the neural pattern so that in a race he can put the three together and maintain this pace for the full quarter.

Occasionally, the quarter-miler should go to the track and run these segments for time, to test his progress. But in the first half of the race-practice period, this shouldn't occur more than once per week. Most running should be done on hilly terrain.

Cross-country running should cease in this period. The athlete should have a sufficient base if he has done it regularly for the six-month conditioning period.

Two types of training should dominate this period. The first, which was just discussed, is this varied combination of fartlek and interval-style running on hills and grass. This should take up about half of the race-practice period.

Mornings

No workouts.

Afternoons

Monday: Surge over segments of approximately 110, 220, 330 and 660 yards for an hour.
Run in place for 10-15 minutes.

Tuesday: 30-60 minutes of intensive lifting with the five basic lifts.
Hang limp on the horizontal bar for two minutes.
Run 4-5 fast runs for a pre-determined amount of time.
Run in place for 5-10 minutes.

Wednesday: Surge over 110-, 220-, 330- and 660-yard segments for an hour.
Run in place for 5-10 minutes.

Thursday: Uphill running for 30-45 minutes.
An hour of gymnastics.
Run in place for 10-15 minutes.

Friday: Run several fast segments for a pre-determined amount of time on a grass track, trying to run farther in each one.
Run in place for 5-10 minutes.

Saturday: Three miles, varied pace.
Run in place for 10-15 minutes.

Sunday: Rest

The other 50% of training should be hard, steady running for the length of time in which the runner expects to run his best race. For example, if he is aiming for a 45-second 440, he would practice running nearly all-out for 45 seconds. He won't be able to make the full 440 (unless his goal is too modest), but should gradually, but steadily, get closer to it.

Gymnastics and weight lifting should continue in this period, but should taper down as the season progresses.

A sample week of training midway through the race-practice period is on page 86.

Competition. Once the serious competitive season starts, training should be curtailed to a few speed sharpening workouts per week.

"Too many athletes don't run enough in the conditioning period and the early part of the race-practice period," Percy said, "then they try to make up for it by exhausting themselves in the competitive season."

If races are run once a week, there should be two or three intensive workouts of short duration each week. If serious racing occurs every few days, then that is all the training the athlete needs. He should have the necessary base to carry him through.

Monday: Surge at full effort over 110, 220, 330 and 660 segments for 30 minutes.
Run in place at fast intervals of 20, 30 and 40 seconds for 4-6 minutes.

Tuesday: Run up a steep hill for 20-40 minutes.
Run in place for 5-10 minutes.

Wednesday: Run two repetitions of all-out running for a pre-determined length of time.
Easy half-mile jog.
Run in place for 5-10 minutes

Thursday: Work on starts for 30 minutes.
Run in place for 5-10 minutes.

Friday: Five wind sprints.

Saturday: Competition.

Sunday: Rest.

Weight lifting, hill training and gymnastics should taper down to one day a week.

Workouts in this period should end with the athlete surging on the spot for 20, 30 and 40 seconds at a time. This will sharpen the athlete's reflexes and increase his accelerating power.

See page 87 for a sample week's schedule.

THE HALF-MILE

To be able to maintain one's basic speed over a full half-mile requires more training volume than for the 440. The conditioning period should contain more mileage, and the race-practice period more and longer intervals per workout.

If the athlete practices long intervals and runs the race in one-third segments, he can build the neural pattern to run the half-mile as a virtual sprint.

The conditioning period. In the conditioning period, the half-miler should run 70-100 miles per week of largely aerobic training.

"If the half-miler does enough work in the conditioning period and learns to run properly, then he can gallop the whole race, Cerutty said.

This running should increase both in terms of distance and in terms of pace as the conditioning period progresses.

Weight lifting should occur three times per week. Other work should include gymnastics, sandhill running and hiking. On the athlete's rest day, he can go swimming.

As with longer distance runners, the half-miler should keep track of his pulse rate, which should slowly decline as the conditioning work takes effect.

A sample week during the half-miler's conditioning period follows:

Mornings

At the beginning of the training year, the half-miler should run 4-7 miles before breakfast three or four days a week. This should steadily increase, to runs of 10 or more miles. They should also increase in frequency, to at least five days per week.

Afternoons

Monday: An hour of intensive weight lifting.
  Hang limp on the horizontal bar for two minutes.
  Run seven miles at a varied pace.
  Run in place for 10-15 minutes.

Tuesday: An hour of gymnastics.
  Eight miles at a varied pace.
  Run in place for 10-15 minutes.

Wednesday: An hour of intensive weight lifting.
  Surging over 440, 660 and 1½-mile segments for an hour.

Thursday: 30-45 minutes of sprinting up a hill with a grade of 1-2.
  Fartlek six miles over varied terrain.
  Run in place for 10 minutes.

Friday: An hour of intensive weight lifting.
  10 miles at a varied pace.

Saturday: One long run of 10-15 miles at a varied pace.

Sunday: Rest.

The race-practice period. Just as with the 440, 880 training is divided up into two primary types: running segments of the race and occasional overdistance intervals, and doing fast runs for the amount of time in which the runner hopes eventually to run his best race. The difference is that the intervals will be longer and there should be more of them.

A sample week during the race-practice period follows:

Mornings

Fartlek running for 2-5 miles early in this period, then taper down and cease entirely in the final weeks.

Afternoons

Monday: An hour of intensive weight lifting.
  Thirty to 45 minutes of surging over 330, 440, 660 and 1½-mile segments.
  Run in place for 10-15 minutes.

Tuesday: Run four intervals of a pre-determined length of time.
  Run in place for 10-15 minutes at a varied pace.

Wednesday: An hour of intensive weight lifting.
  Five miles of surge running.
  Run in place for 5-10 minutes at a varied pace.

Thursday: An hour of surging over 330, 660, 1320 and 1½-mile segments.
  Run in place for 10-15 minutes at a varied pace.

(continued)

(continued from page 89)

Friday: Run several segments at pre-determined time length, trying to run farther on each one.
Gymnastics for 30 minutes.
Run in place for 10-15 minutes.

Saturday: An hour of intensive weight lifting.
Seven miles of varied running.

Sunday: Rest.

Competition. During the peak of the competitive season, the half-miler should limit his running to two or three short but fast speed sharpening workouts per week. Weight lifting and other supplementary work will taper off to one day a week.

A sample week in the competitive period follows:

Monday: Run 330, 440, 660 and 1½-mile surges for 30 minutes.
Run in place for 10-15 minutes.

Tuesday: Run two intervals of a pre-determined time length.
An easy half-mile.
Run in place for 5-10 minutes.

Wednesday: Two miles of varied pace running with several all-out bursts.
Run in place for 10-15 minutes at a varied pace.

Thursday: One mile, easy.
Run in place for 5-10 minutes at a varied pace.

Friday: Rest.

Saturday: Competition.

Sunday: Rest.

Because the 880 demands a greater endurance base than the 440, it should be more of a year-round event. Besides just training more in the conditioning period, the half-miler should regulate all of his aerobic activity in this period. This should include some cross-country running at a varied pace, and such other activities as hiking, biking and swimming.

Except for this endurance base, the two events should be treated similarly. The 880 is not a middle-distance race, and the 440 is not a short sprint.

"Runners train too little for the 440 and too much for the half," Percy said.

He believed that when this situation was resolved, the 440 would easily be galloped in less than 38.0 and the half would be run in 1:30.

Mile and 1500 Meters

Cerutty believed that the modern-day milers, if they used the proper running techniques should be running 3:20. The closest he came was with Elliott.

"The first race I saw Herb Elliott run, in his native state of Western Australia," wrote Percy, "was on Oct. 22, 1955. On a rough grass track like a badly kept football field, I was amazed to see the lad run 4:26 virtually as a solo effort, since no other schoolboy in the race was within 'cooee' of him. I then made the prediction that within three years this lad could run the four-minute mile."

Working with Cerutty just three months, Elliott took his mile best from 4:20.4 (run four months earlier) to 4:06.0. His 4:06, at the Melbourne interclub competition, was a world junior record.

On Feb. 2, 1957, he further lowered the junior mark, running 4:04.4 on a football field, beating future long-distance record setter Ron Clarke.

At the Australian Championships a month later, Elliott ran 4:00.1. Cerutty's prediction had come true. In the same meet, he ran 880 yards in 1:49.3.

"I knew right away that Herb Elliott was the one who could prove my theories and change the future of mile running," Percy said many years later.

In the first month of 1958, at an interclub competition, Elliott broke four minutes, by one-tenth of a second. Five days later, he ran 3:58.7.

At this stage in his career, the world began to take notice, not just of Elliott but of the controversial white-haired man who was his coach. Elliott was written up in all of the top sports periodicals. He received invitations to race in several countries. In May of 1958, he came to California, where he ran five one-mile races in little more than a month.

In the first race, at the Los Angeles Coliseum Stadium, Elliott ran the fastest time ever recorded in America. His 3:57.8 was also the second-best time ever.

Two weeks later, he won a mile race at Modesto in 4:02.7, and then the following weekend, in Compton, he won a much-publicized duel with Ron Delany in the time of 3:58.1.

At the US national championships in Bakersfield, Herb ran a 4:01.4 in his heat, then the next day beat long time Australian rival Merv Lincoln for the championship, with the 3:57.9, just a tenth of a second off his best, run the previous month in Los Angeles.

Cerutty saw little limit to Elliott's potential. He made another prediction that Herb would soon run a 3:55 mile.

On June 8 in Dublin, Ireland, he did even better. He broke the world record by three seconds, clocking 3:54.5.

The demand for the new star was overwhelming. But equally large was the interest in Cerutty. Through his amazing success, Elliott was the runner who gave Percy public exposure.

Herb said it was Percy who showed him the path to his goal, "but after I'd gone some of the way, I didn't need prodding anymore. There is the point of no return, where you have labored for so long, sacrificed so much that you can't go back. You must reach your goal and trample on anyone who tries to stop you. Afterward, when you have made it, when you're sitting on top of the world, perhaps you need the prodding again to ensure you don't fall off your perch."

A month after his world record mile, Elliott ran an 8:37.6 two-mile, finishing second to Albert Thomas, another Cerutty-trained runner, who set a world record of 8:32.0.

Cerutty had by this time reached a full public exposure. Already, public reaction seemed to fall mainly in two categories: genius and eccentric.

On Aug. 28, 1958, at Gothenberg, Sweden, Herb Elliott set a world record in the 1500 meters with 3:36.0.

Elliott's most successful year was probably 1958. He set two world records, and improved his best times in the half-mile and two-mile.

Herb Elliott's schedule trained him both mentally and physically. As he was running, particularly during varied, fartlek-style running, he would imagine other runners were approaching to pass, and he would speed up and slow down. This was how Cerutty thought the mile should be run.

Elliott's training during the conditioning period:

Monday: morning—seven miles, varied pace;
afternoon—circuit running (long cross-country intervals);
evening—easy five miles.

Tuesday: morning—five miles, varied pace;
afternoon—repeat hill training;
evening—weight training.

Wednesday: morning—seven miles;
afternoon—six miles, varied running and sprinting.

Thursday: morning—seven miles, varied pace;
afternoon—15 miles.

Friday: rest.

Saturday: morning—five miles, varied pace;
afternoon—weight training;
evening—five miles, varied running and sprinting.

Sunday: morning: six miles;
afternoon: intervals, golf course.

In 1959, Herb didn't surpass any of his records (although he ran 3:55.4 in London, the second-fastest mile ever). Perhaps what he had said about needing prodding once you have attained greatness was being proven.

"I felt before the 1960 Games that I needed Percy's

inspiration more than I could remember needing it when I was a young and dedicated athlete," Herb wrote.

He was dedicated in the Rome Olympic 1500 meters. He ran the first 400 meters in 58.2, clocked 1:57.8 at the 800 and finished in world record of 3:35.6. His closest competitor was 24-year-old Michel Jazy of France, who, five years later, would break the world mile record. Elliott's time was the equivalent of a 3:52 mile.

"No other athlete has approached Elliott," Cerutty said. "It will be tragic for athletics if Elliott's studies and his obligations involved in earning a livelihood prevent the development of his full powers and possibilities."

But Elliott was tiring of the rigors of running around the world. He wrote of the post-Olympic touring:

"The cumulative effect of traveling and racing a series of fast times—I'd been on the move since early May—was starting to become apparent. A group of friends had offered to pay for my flight from Stockholm to London and arrange private accommodations in London if I'd agree to run in an invitational mile during the athletics match between London and Warsaw at White City on Sept. 3. Although by now my only real desire was to get home and be reunited with my family and Anne, I could not have left Europe until after Sept. 5, when I was committed to run at Oslo, and so I agreed to fill in the time by going to London."

Even before, but especially after, he was in such demand that it became hard for him to run without pressure. To please the demand of promoters, he ran a series of exhibition races but lacked the fierce spirit of earlier races. Still, he won them all.

When Elliott retired from running, to pursue his current career in West Germany for Shell Oil Company, Cerutty's techniques were somewhat abandoned. Elliott had been the one to bring them to public attention, but with his retirement, Cerutty's

The classic running style of Herb Elliott: absence of shoulder sway, low arm carriage, relaxed power.

potential was also, temporarily at least, retiring.

Percy's ideas touched all areas of track and field, but their true test came in the mile. The mile was the event that he centered his concentration on, largely because of Herb Elliott who applied himself more than any of the other athletes.

"You might be able to run faster," Cerutty once told Elliott, "but you won't be able to run any harder."

Having the right pupil was what Percy needed and found with Elliott. "'Fix your goal and work for it,' says Percy Cerutty, and I fixed mine," Herb wrote. "I wanted to be the best miler in the world."

The two had a unique relationship, based on a mutual dedication to excellence. Herb used to meditate on his neural patterns for his race by sitting beneath a tree and thinking about running, while Percy sprinted back and forth in front of him. This was approximately two hours before the race. Afterward, they would return to the hotel room, where Elliott would take a short nap and eat a small salad.

He would never think specifically about his competition and their best times. Percy knew that many athletes went through this process and literally talked themselves out of victory. They become frightened and panic mentally.

All of the top milers must learn to relax in order to

avoid this, especially since there is often more attention, and pressure, on the mile than on other events.

John Walker cited this as a reason for his success in the 1976 Olympics, where he won a gold medal in the 1500 meters. "I think a lot of athletes panicked before the Olympic Games and did too much. I had one of my worst build-ups, but it didn't worry me because I knew I had three hard years going for me. It was all a matter of getting ready. I didn't panic."

Percy would hide Elliott in a quiet spot in the stadium before races, so that people couldn't find him and disturb his concentration with questions about the upcoming race.

Elliott shows perfect form on the last lap of his 1960 Olympic 1500, which he won in world-record time.

THE 3:20 MILE

The training and racing techniques that Elliott used could be carried on to tremendous possibilities. Cerutty believed that if they were properly developed, he would see a 3:20 mile within his lifetime. But in the early 1970s, particularly when he came to the United States on a lecture tour in 1974, he spoke of how the modern-day athlete had failed to carry on where Elliott left off. He still saw huge improvement when the athlete runs with the proper galloping movement.

"Cerutty compares this running style with that of a horse," wrote the *Denver Post* on June 2, 1974, "and claims that if and when his techniques are learned, accepted and adopted, 'some bloke is going to run the mile, not in 3:50, but in 3:20!'"

Even the advancement the mile went through with Jim Ryun, Filbert Bayi and John Walker is just a fraction of what it should be, Percy believed.

Cerutty thought that the four-minute miler who utilized his running techniques could, in six years, run a 3:20 mile. The plan was designed for the miler to run just under four minutes the first year, 3:55 the next, 3:50 the third year, 3:40 the next, 3:30 the fifth and, finally, 3:20.

It would involve large quantities of long endurance running and weight lifting during the conditioning period, and progressively faster intervals on the grass and sand during the race-practice period. But most importantly, it involved the athlete learning the proper, natural way to run, utilizing his lungs, developing the five basic movements and lengthening his stride. It would take six years to learn this, to create the proper neural patterns. The conditioning period should be used for this, for improving one's running style.

Building the proper neural pattern for running as fast as 3:20 is a gradual process of running segments of the race at an increasingly faster pace. For instance, this is the progression of going from 3:55 to 3:50 to 3:40. The runner should start out running

FIRST YEAR

Interval	First Month	Second Month	Third Month
220	35.0	32.5	30.0
330	52.5	48.7	45.0
440	70.0	65.0	60.0
660	1:45.0	1:37.5	1:30.0
880	2:20.0	2:10.0	2:00.0
	4:40 mile pace	4:20 mile pace	4:00 mile pace

SECOND YEAR

Interval	First Month	Second Month	Third Month
220	32.5	30.0	29.0
330	48.7	45.0	43.0
440	65.0	60.0	58.7
660	1:37.5	1:30.0	1:27.5
880	2:10	2:00.0	1:57.4
	4:20 mile pace	4:00 mile pace	3:55 mile pace

THIRD YEAR

Interval	First Month	Second Month	Third Month
220	30.0	29.0	28.7
330	45.0	43.0	42.0
440	60.0	58.7	57.4
660	1:30.0	1:27.7	1:26.0
880	2:00.0	1.57.4	1:54.8
	4:00 mile pace	3:55 mile pace	3:50 mile pace

FOURTH YEAR

Interval	First Month	Second Month	Third Month
220	29.0	28.7	27.5
330	43.0	42.0	41.0
440	58.7	57.4	55.0
660	1:27.7	1:26.0	1:22.5
880	1:57.4	1:54.8	1:50
	3:55 mile pace	3:50 mile pace	3:40 mile pace

FIFTH YEAR

Interval	First Month	Second Month	Third Month
220	28.7	27.5	26.2
330	42.0	41.0	39.3
440	57.4	55.0	52.5
660	1:26.0	1:22.5	1:18.7
880	1:54.8	1:50.0	1:45.0
	3:50 mile pace	3:40 mile pace	3:30 mile pace

SIXTH YEAR

Interval	First Month	Second Month	Third Month
220	27.5	26.2	25.0
330	41.0	39.3	37.5
440	55.0	52.5	50.0
660	1:22.5	1:18.7	1:15.0
880	1:50.0	1:45.0	1:40.0
	3:40 mile pace	3:30 mile pace	3:20 mile pace

220s in 29, 330s in 43, 440s in 58.7, 660s in 1:27.7, 880s in 1:57.4. Then to take it down to 3:50, his training times should be 28.7, 42.0, 57.4, 1:26.6 and 1:54.8. For 3:40, interval times should be 27.5, 41.0, 55.0, 1:22.5 and 1:50.

The progression to 3:20 demands steadily increased volume during the conditioning period, as well as hill training and weight work.

Ideally, in each of the six race-practice periods, the progression of intervals should follow a regular pattern (see page 99).

This was obviously an ambitious program, since running 1:40 half-miles in practice is today all but inconceivable. But in the context of this program, it has never been tested.

It also seems more regimented than most of Percy's training ideas, but actually these intervals were only one part of a varied training scheme, and should occur no more than twice a week.

Whether anyone will use this training program remains to be seen. If someone does, the mile record will plummet. If not, it will dribble down to 3:20 over a period of many decades.

In the 10 years following Herb Elliott's retirement, the mile mark was only cut by a little more than three seconds. Percy believed it should have been in the vicinity of 3:40 or below by that time. But no miler had grasped his techniques, no one had applied the dedication that Elliott did. Although the conditioning period is crucial, Cerutty didn't think there was one plan applicable to all.

"This may be satisfactory for those 'triers' who need a concise primer: a detailed blueprint," he said. "and I must reiterate that success does not lie in any such things. The ease with which schedules can be written, the demand for them, and the readiness of certain types of coaches to supply them—I can only say, if it was that easy, any successful coach could make a fortune."

The only universal idea for this period is that the athlete should build an endurance base, should make

Herb Elliott strengthens himself on the horizontal bar. He did a full range of activities besides running.

sure not to lose enjoyment of running (if running becomes boring, he should take off a few days and go hiking) and do supplementary exercises such as gymnastics, hill running and weight lifting. The conditioning period should be one of experimenting, particularly with developing the proper movements.

"The athlete should learn to be his own coach during the conditioning period," Cerutty said.

Race-practice. Several types of workouts should be run during this period. Timed intervals, preferably on the grass, should be run once or twice a week.

There should be a fair amount of variation during this period to prevent staleness. None of the running should be at a steady pace. There should always be variety. One workout that several Cerutty athletes did was running hard intervals on the grass for 10 minutes, then slowly until recovered, and then another hard 10 minutes. Some athletes kept this up for thirty minutes to an hour.

The athlete should be careful that he doesn't wear himself down in this period. Long runs should come only once a week and should be followed by at least one day of easy running.

Approximately 80% of training should be run

at race pace. This is to condition the runner, mentally as well as physically, for fast racing. As the race-practice period evolves, so should training speed. Intervals and grass running should be run increasingly faster.

But though these should be run steadily faster, the pace should ebb and flow. The runner should practice varying the pace, surging, dropping back, etc.

"The top miles of the future will be run at an uneven pace," Percy said.

Once serious racing is underway, training should be almost all quality work. An endurance base should be built in, and endurance work such as long-distance running and weight lifting can be ceased.

Racing. All training should have two purposes in relation to training. It should physically condition the athlete to run faster, and it should reinforce and sharpen neural patterns to run faster.

Australian Olympian Jenny Orr runs with proper style.

"If training has been successful, racing should be too," Cerutty said. "It is an improper attitude that rationalizes a very sub-par performance off to a bad day." Although Elliott had worse days than others, he never lost at the mile or metric mile. The trouble with accepting a poor performance as just the result of a bad day is that it ignores the reasons for the poor performance and makes it easier to fall back on that excuse when the runner is feeling tired in a race.

"Stay away from the pressure and run the best race you can," Percy advised his milers.

The runner should never worry about the other competitors or their previous times or performances. This will take a great deal of practice for some people. For others, it comes fairly naturally.

The runner should make himself think about the pure act of running before a race, not the specific race coming up, or any previous race. He should stay away from question-asking reporters and try to be as relaxed as possible before the race. Elliott was so relaxed he took one-hour naps before some of his greatest races.

Percy believed that, ideally, the runner should not develop one strategy that he always uses. He should vary it as much as possible. Zatopek discussed this with Cerutty in 1952. His varied arm movements and surges pointed that way to proper distance running.

"An even pace is not the most economical," Percy said. "This is a misconception. Energy isn't steady. It comes and goes in bursts, and the runner should go with it when it comes. The zombie-like, steady movements of most middle-distance runners completely ignores this natural process. The runner has to take advantage of the natural flow of energy."

The purpose of a racing situation is to express the neural patterns that were connected by running segments during the race-practice period.

"The athlete should be aroused simply by the idea of competition," Percy said. "This should be enough to make him emotionally ready, and draw on what has been developed through practice."

This arousal can be hampered by worry about the race or the competition, lack of interest or staleness. These are the enemies of good racing. An athlete can put in months of gruelling, exacting workouts and then be defeated by them in a race situation. Elliott was almost immune to them, but most runners have a harder time of it.

When serious racing season is underway, races take priority. Training should be limited as much as possible, usually to no more than a little sharpening work on the grass. The runner has to save his best efforts for the race. Many waste them in time trials and workouts.

If the runner has trained properly and is "mentally tough," the race should be run as fast as possible. Since the runner's physical condition doesn't change very significantly in the space of a week or two, if the runner is doing his best, his racing times should not fluctuate much from race to race. They should be progressively faster.

Some runners have been known to experience wide fluctuations. Jim Ryun's best mile time varied by as much as 20 seconds one season.

Percy believed that the athlete should always give everything he has. "Always be prepared to meet any challenge anytime," he would say.

At the end of the race, the runner should know he has run to the best of his abilities. If he does not feel this, he is missing the purpose of racing.

Herb Elliott always gave his best. Before his first US race in 1958, Herb had been sightseeing each day in the Los Angeles area for almost a week straight. He hadn't been running much or sleeping much, and by race day was tired both mentally and physically. His opponent, Merv Lincoln, saw this and tried to burn him out. But Herb summoned his reserves in the race and gave it all he had to win in 3:57.8.

This is what top miling should be: an all-out performance each time. The athlete should concentrate on doing his best; everything else is extraneous. "Psyching out," "psyching up," thinking about the other competitors and worrying about strategy are all extraneous.

Since Elliott, no miler has developed the proper theories of running. If they had, we would have a 3:40 mile easily.

Whether the 3:40 mile, or the 3:20 mile, will happen anytime soon can't be predicted. Percy believed it possible in a very short time. He wanted to see a four-minute miler devote six years to his theories. He realized he wouldn't live to see it but hoped that his theories would live to create the 3:20 mile.

5000 and 10,000 Meters

The three-mile and six-mile (or 5000 and 10,000 meters) is the most compatible double in track and field, with the possible exception of the 100 and 220 (or 100 and 200 meters). Such Olympic champions as Nurmi, Kolehmainen, Zatopek, Mimoun, Kuts and Viren are the best examples of athletes who have mastered this double.

However, if the athlete is running just one of the two events, his training should be different for each, because there is an inherent difference in the two. In fact, some three-milers double in the mile and some six-milers double in the marathon.

The main difference in training for these two events is one of volume. The six-miler should run longer intervals and more fast, varied-pace runs.

The endurance base for these two events is possibly the most efficient one in track and field. This is why many runners of these distances make better marathoners than those who train specifically for the marathon. Many marathon specialists are primarily concerned with mileage; the three- and six-milers average a lot of miles, but they are done at a faster tempo.

"The three- and six-mile type has one of the best endurance backgrounds in track and field," Percy said, "especially if he does gymnastics and hill work."

The three- and six-miler should be a combination of strength and speed. Percy said that the top six-miler should be able to run a fast mile in any part of his race. Many runners who attempt this pacing tactic can't pull it off because they lack the conditioning.

"Vladimir Kuts was the best runner who could run with these tactics. Unless the athlete has the proper strength, this tactic only wastes energy," said Percy.

When the runner has this strength, he can practically dictate the outcome of a race. These fast bursts can destroy the tactics of other runners. For this strategy to work, the best position to be in is the front or on the side of the pack of runners.

A more recent example of a good tactical runner is the US's multi-record holder Steve Prefontaine.

Murray Halberg, winner of the 1960 Olympics 5000-meter race, had a tremendous amount of strength. If he had been able to use his left arm, which was virtually paralyzed, he might have been the greatest distance runner ever.

"Some people say that arm movement is not important and think that Murray Halberg is the proof," Percy said. "I say had he had full use of both arms, he could have been the best distance runner of all time."

TRAINING

The three- and six-milers should both build a high-mileage base. But these shouldn't be plodding miles; they should be run at a fast, varied pace. The differences between the two events are not great, but the runner should pick just one to concentrate on.

"No athlete should train to be great at several events," Percy said. "He should train to be great at just one, but do so in a way that he can at least be very good in several others."

The conditioning period. For both events, the conditioning period should contain a great deal of mileage, as much as 100 miles per week. This should be accomplished in two workouts per day during the week and one workout on Saturday.

The three- and six-miler should basically do the same training throughout the conditioning period. It isn't until the race-practice period that training for the two becomes particularly specialized.

The first half of the conditioning period should be spent building to the point where the runner can go 15-20 miles at a varied pace without much difficulty. Once this is done, the runner should begin to concentrate on running faster.

"The important thing in this period," Percy said, "is to gradually work up to the point where you can run 20 miles at a varied pace with faster times. This type of progressive training will slowly lower the runner's basic pulse rate down to 40 beats and build a strong secondary tank of energy and strength."

The runner's mileage should vary each day. There should be one day each week when the athlete rests.

A sample week midway through the conditioning period follows:

Mornings

Each morning, the runner should cover a distance of 3-10 miles. This amount should increase proportionately as the conditioning period evolves.

Afternoons

Monday: 30-60 minutes of intensive weight lifting.
Hang limp on the horizontal bar for two minutes.
Fartlek, seven miles.
Run in place for 10-15 minutes.

Tuesday: An hour of gymnastics.
Thirty to 45 minutes of uphill sprinting.
Run in place for 10-15 minutes.

Wednesday: 30-60 minutes of intensive weight lifting.
Hang limp on the horizontal bar for two minutes.
Fartlek, eight miles.
Run in place for 10-15 minutes.

Thursday: 15 miles of varied pace running.

Friday: 30-60 minutes of intensive weight lifting.
Hang limp on the horizontal bar for two minutes.
Fartlek, three miles.
Run in place for 10-15 minutes.

Saturday: 18 miles of varied pace running.

Sunday: Rest.

Several times during the conditioning period, there should be a "60-mile weekend." This consists of running four sessions of approximately 15 miles each on Saturday and Sunday.

Gymnastics, hill training and weight lifting should supplement this running.

The race-practice period. In this period, the runner should begin to develop the proper neural pattern for the times he's going to concentrate on. This can be done by running segments of the event at race pace or slightly faster.

A sample week midway through the race-practice period follows:

Mornings

30-45 minutes of intensive weight lifting 2-3 times a week.
3-mile: 3-6 miles at a varied pace.
6-mile: 4-8 miles at a varied pace.

Afternoons

Monday: *3-mile:* 5 one-mile intervals at faster than race pace with easy running in between.
Run in place for 10-15 minutes.
6-mile: 4 two-mile intervals at faster than race pace.
Run in place for 10-15 minutes.

Tuesday: *3-mile:* An hour of uphill sprints.
Two miles at a varied pace.
Run in place for 10-15 minutes.
6-mile: An hour of uphill sprints.
5 miles at a varied pace.
Run in place for 10-15 minutes.

Wednesday: *3-mile:* 8 miles at a varied pace with 110, 220, 330, 440 and 660 surges.
6-mile: 12 miles at a varied pace with 220, 330, 660 and 800 surges.

Thursday: *3-mile:* 1½ hours of varied pace running. including six 660 surges.
Run in place for 10-15 minutes.
6-mile: 1½ hours of varied pace running including six 880 yard surges.

Friday: *3-mile:*Six two-mile intervals with easy running in between.
Run in place for 10-15 minutes.
6-mile: 5 three-mile intervals with easy running in between.
Run in place for 10-15 minutes.

Saturday: 20 miles at a varied pace.

Sunday: Rest.

Running these segments at varied paces in the course of a long run teaches the runner to use surge tactics in a race.

"It takes a lot of cardiovascular strength, stamina and endurance to run one hard interval after another for three miles or more," Cerutty said. "Only when the athlete has built in a strong secondary tank and has the strength from six months of proper conditioning can he do these surge tactics successfully. The basic idea in the race-practice period is to run at a fast rate over segments of the race and then to tie them together in a time trial or race. The world class three-miler and six-miler should be able to run a fast mile during any part of his race without significant loss of speed or energy over the remaining laps of the race."

Competition. During the final weeks of the competitive season, the three- and six-miler should work mostly on speed sharpening. He could practice surging tactics regularly in this period by running up and down hills that are not as steep as the big hill he uses in the conditioning period.

A classic example of this surging, breakaway tactic was the performance of Vladimir Kuts of the Soviet Union in the 5000- and 10,000-meter runs at the 1956 Olympics. His surging, irregular pace devastated the rest of the field. Emil Zatopek is the other runner who typified this strategy.

Percy wrote a poem about Kuts as he watched him in the Olympic stadium and later said, "Kuts showed how 5000- and 10,000-meter runners should run their race. His breakaway tactics were much more natural and effective than the other runners' strategies in the race."

These breakaway tactics should be developed by running 330, 440, 660 and 880 surges in training. They should be tiring but never exhausting. Leslie Perry, the first distance runner Cerutty coached (he represented Australia in the 1952 Olympics by running against Emil Zatopek in the 5000- and 10,000-meter runs), was an example of a runner who

(Left-right) Leslie Perry, Geoff Warren and Dave Stephens all were Cerutty-trained.

exhausted himself too much between races and couldn't reach his potential because of it.

"Les Perry would run such hard 10-mile efforts during the week that they would practically put him in a coma for a couple days," Cerutty said. "Any unnecessary stress put on the runner in this part of the season will only detract from his competitive performance."

In the competitive period, weight training, gymnastics and hill running should be done weekly.

Like a marathoner, the three- and six-miler should keep up his conditioning in the non-running season with hiking, some cross-country running, swimming and bicycling.

The endurance base should then be built up again with the start of the conditioning period.

Said Percy, "The endurance built up for the three- and six-mile should be so thorough that the runner comes into the competition season able to compete in almost any long-distance event."

10

The Marathon

Over the past several years, the marathon has become the most popular running event in the world. Yet there are still few athletes who are able to reach their potential in this event because of the predominant plodding style of training.

The athlete who has conditioned himself for the six-mile is generally a better marathoner than the runner who has trained specifically for the longer race. The reason is simple. The six-miler trains at a faster pace. This is what most marathoners neglect. They think the key word is *volume*, and add up their mileage, while ignoring the truly important aspect, *intensity*. Plodding along at a slow pace in practice only conditions the runner to plod along. It also teaches him to run in an inefficient, unnatural style. Emil Zatopek is the classic example of the runner who trained for the 5000- and 10,000-meter races, and excelled in the marathon. The coordination of movement needed to run a marathon at five minutes per mile will never be developed if the runner trains at six- or seven-minute pace.

The basic plan for a marathoner is first to build an endurance base through running, hiking and weight lifting. The marathoner should run with the basic movements, building his endurance to the point where he can run a full marathon distance and then 30 miles in practice.

Once this base has been established, the marathoner should begin to concentrate on speed. A hundred miles per week of jogging will never allow the runner to reach his full potential. If he cuts his mileage down to 60 but runs them faster than he would for 100 miles, he will get much more benefit.

The marathoner should predetermine the rate he wants to run his race, then do much of his training at this speed. For instance, if he wants to run the distance at a six-minute pace, he should practice five- and 10-mile runs at this pace. This is similar in principle of developing neural patterns for the sprints or middle distances, but it should evolve beyond mere segments. There should be a gradual build-up; first the runner should practice five-mile runs at a given pace, then eight miles at the same pace, then 10, 15, etc.

Most of this training should not be on road surfaces. This damages a runner's legs, shortens his stride and confines his movement. Training should be on grass, sand or soft dirt as much as possible.

"The hard surfaces that are made by man will shorten the runner's stride to a pitifully restricted gait and turn him into a slow plodder," Cerutty said. "There are no hard roads in nature. Running on hard roads year after year will eventually cripple the athlete for life. Running on cement, asphalt or any other hard surface not only shortens the stride and turns the runner into a plodder, but it also inhibits any creative expression the athlete originally had as a marathon runner. It turns him into a zombie. Many race organizers seem to forget that the marathon and other long road races, of 60-100 miles even, were originally run over country roads of sand and dirt. This is the natural way of running long-distance races."

TRAINING FOR THE MARATHON

The Conditioning Period. Before the runner can improve his speed in the marathon, he should first be able to run the full distance. The early part of the conditioning period should be devoted to this. It is ridiculous for a runner to total large mileage weeks

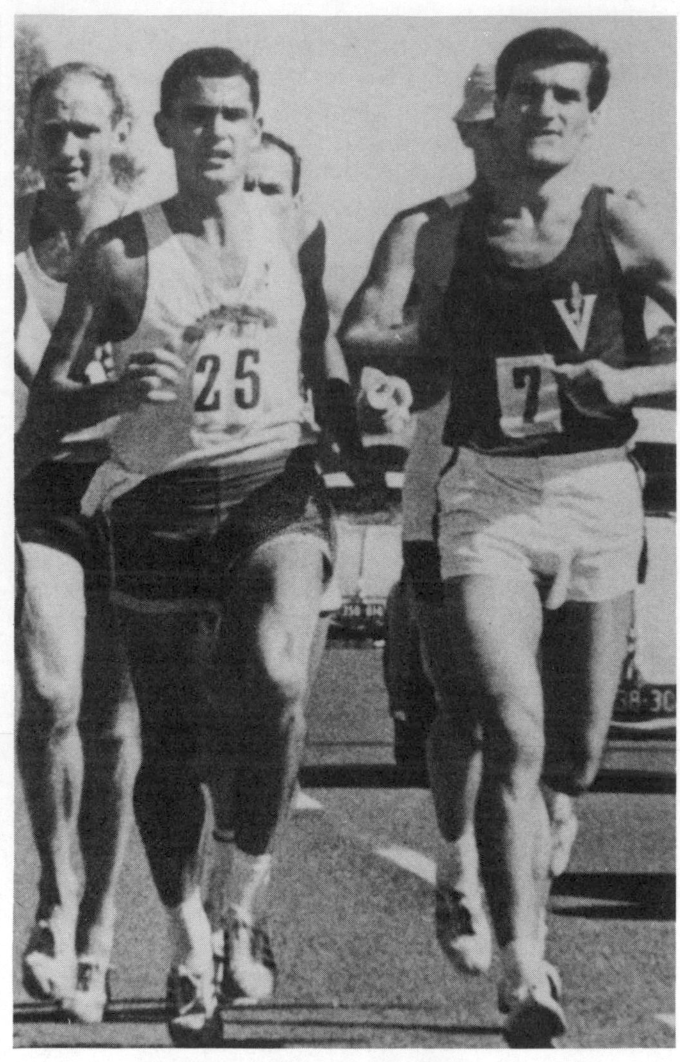

Ron Clarke (left) and Derek Clayton.

without ever running close to a full marathon in practice. Even if a runner puts in more than 100 miles per week, if he does so by adding up eight- and 10-mile runs, he is not equipping his body, either physically or mentally, to cope with the full 26.

The early conditioning period should not be based on miles per week; it should be on building to the point where the runner can run a full marathon and beyond (up to 30 miles) in practice. Speed work should come later. This build-up shouldn't be done by trying to run farther each day; it should be done very gradually, with easy days separating those in which the runner increases his distance. This training idea predicted the hard-easy theory of running such coaches as Bill Bowerman (1972 U.S. Olympic coach) have since made commonplace.

Although this build-up doesn't involve speed training, it is important that the runner doesn't lapse into a slow, plodding pace. He should vary his movements as he runs, with some occasional fast bursts, although the overall pace should remain considerably slower than the eventual race pace. Hill training and weight training should supplement this build-up to ensure the athlete develops proper strength.

Percy believed there should be short rest periods in the course of a distance run. For example, a 10-mile run might be broken into a series of two-, three- and five-mile sections. Each section should be run at varied pace with some fartlek-style running.

"In concentrating on a sub-five-minute per mile pace, the runner should first build up to 30 miles of easy running in the conditioning period," Cerutty said. "This should not be fast, but it should not be plodding, either. The runner should build up to this by running first five miles, then building up to 10, to 15, to 20 and so on. These should be done in segments of varied speeds over grass. The run should be broken up into two-mile, three-mile and five-mile segments. Between each one, the runner should trot, canter, gallop and ease into a steady gait with a modified canter."

This set of distances shouldn't be planned. It should evolve from the way the runner feels. This is the same principle behind fartlek. These segments, as well as the varied running within them, are all steps in avoiding the common temptation to plod along at a slow, steady pace.

A sample week while the athlete is building to 30 miles is as follows:

Monday
Morning: Intensive weight lifting for 30-40 minutes;
Hang limp on the horizontal bar for three minutes.
Afternoon: Five miles, in two segments of varied tempo running;
Six uphill sprints.

Tuesday
Morning: Gymnastics for 30-40 minutes.
Afternoon: 15 miles in five segments of varied running.

Wednesday
Afternoon: Varied tempo running and surging for 5-10 miles;
Intensive weight lifting for 45 minutes.

Thursday
Morning: Easy running for five miles with several surges.
Afternoon: 18 miles in five segments of varied running.

Friday
Morning: Eight-mile hike.
Afternoon: Easy one-mile runs with surges; 30 to 40 minutes of hill running

Saturday
Morning: 22 miles in six segments of varied running.
Afternoon: 30-40 minutes of intensive weight lifting.

Sunday
Rest.

This is a sample week in the second month of the conditioning period. Each week should be different, as the runner progresses closer to his 30-mile goal, which he should achieve by the third month of conditioning.

Training should always include one rest day per week to allow the organism to recover. In the middle, and again at the end, of the conditioning period, there should be a three-day rest from all running.

Running should never end for the day with the athlete in a dragging, half-exhausted state. It should end strong so the runner learns not to give up in a racing situation.

"The marathon runner should finish by 'whipping in' his training runs," Percy said. "He should never loaf in like a tired dog. Each individual section of a training run should be finished strong. The athlete must form the neural pattern in his brain to run fast in a race, and the only way he can do this is to run fast in practice. A fast final half-mile at the end of each training section must become a conditioned response."

THE CONDITIONING PERIOD

Once the marathoner has achieved a 30-mile run, which should occur midway through the conditioning period, he has reached a transition point. His program should begin to change, no longer concentrating on reaching the long distance, but in running it fast. This should be the focus of the last half and, particularly, the last third of the conditioning period.

A month-by-month plan of objectives for the conditioning period follows:

First month. Beginning with short-distance runs, the marathoner should begin to establish an endurance base. Weight lifting should be introduced right away. Long, fartlek runs should steadily increase in distance, separated by easy days of short runs and some supplementary exercise such as hiking or gymnastics.

By the end of the first month, the runner should have built to 12-15 miles without a great deal of difficulty. This can be done by taking an eight-mile run the first week, a 10 the second and a 12 the third.

Second month. In the second month, supplementary work should increase, not the volume but the intensity. Long runs at a varied pace should continue to increase in distance with two such runs each week. At the end of the second month, the runner should be able to run close to 20 miles. He shouldn't try to do much more than 20, since this is so early, and he can become mentally tired if he builds too fast. Being able to run 17-20 is sufficient.

Third month. By the end of the third month, the marathoner should be able to run more than 20 miles at a varied pace without a great deal of difficulty. He should continue to run in two-, three- and five-mile segments of fartlek-style running.

Fourth month. This is the month the marathoner

should be able to run 30 miles, in the same varied-pace, segment running as the rest of training. Resistance work should also increase.

Fifth month. Once the runner is able to run 30 miles, he should begin to work on running it at varied speeds and paces. The runner should begin running at the pace he wants to race at, starting with five- and 10-mile runs. By the end of the fifth month, he should be running 1/2-3/4 of the distance at race pace. Running speed should still vary considerably in the course of a single run, but the overall time should be faster. There should still be one long run a week, at slower than race pace.

Sixth month. In the final month of the conditioning period, the marathoner should be able to run three-quarters of the distance at race pace. In addition, he should practice running one-half of it at faster than race pace and 1-1/4 of it at slower than race pace. This is the last month of building volume, so it should be the highest mileage month of the conditioning period. Weight training and other non-running work should also reach a peak during this month.

In each stage of training, long runs should be separated by short runs. One day each week should be a rest day when the athlete swims or hikes but doesn't do any running. Total mileage should never exceed 400 per month.

RACE PRACTICE AND COMPETITION

The conditioning period may extend into the race-practice, as the runner continues to build toward running the full marathon distance at race pace. But there should also be the introduction of some interval work and more hill training. Since the marathon is such a taxing event, the athlete shouldn't run more than 3-4 in a season, and the first one may come after the end of the race-practice period. To stay sharp, shorter races such as 5000- and 10,000-meter track races and various length road races should be run.

Weight lifting, gymnastics and other resistance exercise should continue to supplement the distance work in the early part of the race-practice period.

Running training should have two objectives in this period: (1) to build up to running the full distance at race pace and (2) to build up running faster than race pace.

Gradually, interval running should be implemented, though on grass if possible. This includes 220, 330, 440, 660 and 880 segments, and occasional intervals of 1-3 miles. These should be run faster than race pace, although not as if training for a mile. For instance, the marathoner who hopes to run at a five-minute mile pace should run his intervals as follows: 220s in 30-35, 330s in 48-52, 440s in 65-70, 660s in 1:40-1:50 and 880s in 2:18-2:25.

One day each week should be a non-running day when the athlete participates in some other activity.

A typical week of workouts in the first month of the race-practice period follows:

Monday
Morning: Intensive weight lifting for 30-40 minutes.
Afternoon: Five miles of fartlek running

Tuesday
Afternoon: Surge over a series of 440s, with easy running between each burst, for an hour and a half.

Wednesday
Morning: One hour of gymnastics
Afternoon: 15 miles, varied running.

Thursday
Afternoon: Hill running for 30 minutes;
Five miles, fartlek;
A half-hour of intensive weight lifting.

Friday
Morning: 18 miles at varied speed, with overall rate race pace or faster.

Saturday
Morning: Intensive weight lifting.
Afternoon: 880 surging, varied running, 12 miles total.

Sunday
Rest.

Cerutty believed many top athletes could maintain a 4:40 per mile pace over the marathon distance if they trained properly. This would yield a 2:03 marathon (the current record is 2:08:33).

"Marathoners are mostly plodders in their training," Cerutty said. "How can they hope to run five minutes per mile races if they run six- or seven-minute miles in practice? Most marathoners believe that all they have to do is run, run, run. This plodding only destroys the individual strengths a runner had at the start of his athletic career.

"If they trained properly, so that they built to 30 miles in the conditioning period, then to running that 30 miles *fast*, they could be running the marathon at 4:40 pace or faster."

Ideally, two marathon races should come in a three- or four-month season. The first should be midway through the race-practice period, and the second should be at the very end. Between these should be shorter track races to reinforce the neural patterns for the differents segments of the marathon.

During the second half of the race-practice period, weight lifting, hill running and gymnastics should taper down to one day per week.

Training in this final period should be almost exclusively at race pace or faster. There should be three long, hard runs a week at varied pace with all five of the basic movements. The runs should still be divided into two-, three- and five-mile segments just as in the conditioning period, only by this time they should be faster. This is consistent with the idea of intensive training that Cerutty advocated for all realms of exercise.

In the main competitive season, mileage should be limited to about 40-50 per week. But this should be composed of two or three intensive distance runs of 10-20 miles, one of which should include interval running on the grass. A track or road race may be substituted for any of these intense training runs.

Training in the final month before the marathon should be as follows:

Monday: Eighteen miles, faster than race pace, by covering series of two-, three- and five-mile segments with the five basic movements; finish by running in place at a fast pace for five minutes.

Tuesday: Ten miles of varied running, at overall race pace.

Wednesday: An hour and a half of 440 intervals on the grass, or fartlek running.

Thursday: Fifteen miles in segments at faster than race pace; run in place for 10 minutes.

Friday: Easy three-mile run with bursts.

Saturday: Competition.

Sunday: Rest

If the runner has followed this program faithfully, he shouldn't have a great deal of difficulty running the marathon at the designated race pace.

The endurance developed through building to a 30-mile run in the conditioning period should build in a reserve tank which will carry the runner at a steady pace through the final miles of the race.

"In the conditioning period and the first part of the race-practice period," Cerutty said, "the marathoner should build in a strong secondary tank that will carry him through the final stages of a race at a fast pace. This fast pace comes when the runner practices running segments of the marathon at faster than race pace."

The marathon differs from the other running events in that it is not one that can be run every week, two weeks or even every month. The preparation and recovery involved requires that the runner limit his marathon racing to two or three a year. Few top marathoners run more than 3-4 races in a single year.

Once obvious difficulty with dividing a marathoner's schedule into a half-year conditioning period and three month race-practice period is that marathon scheduling is not this uniform. There is no "season" for the marathon as there is for other events. There are big races throughout the year. For this reason, the conditioning and race-practice schedule is more applicable to a runner who is peaking for a specific race, such as the Olympics (or the Olympic trials and then the Olympics). However, one shouldn't run them at even intervals throughout the year, such as every four months, and expect to perform better in each one.

There should be a full six-month conditioning period in which the emphasis is on building endurance, not a speed, base. After he has built to 30 miles, a marathoner might want to run a marathon in the conditioning period. But he shouldn't cram in speed training for it. This throws the program off and defeats the purpose of the conditioning period. Cerutty believed that all athletes should be "prepared to meet any challenge at any time," but he also saw the need for dividing the training year into conditioning, race-practice and competition periods. The length of each period may vary slightly with each athlete and his goals, but these two essential training periods must be maintained.

Training for the marathon shouldn't be limited to nine months per year, as for other events. The marathoner should run all year, with one nine-month period and the other three months for building his neural pattern for specific races.

If a runner began training in the fall during a pre-Olympic year, he might want to run one winter marathon, then move into the halfway point of the race-practice period for his country's trial and build from there to the Olympic race.

When marathoners learn to adopt a schedule such as Percy advocated, barriers like two hours, which today seem almost unreachable, may be surpassed.

"Marathoners are almost all plodders," Percy said. "They think the only thing that matters is *how much* they run, rather than *how* they run. There are many good marathon runners today. But when the proper movements and programs are learned, that is when we will see the true potential of the marathon."

III

THE SPECIAL EVENTS

11

Throwing and Jumping

Cerutty's theories of full-lung aeration and natural movement are applicable to the jumping and throwing events, though he seldom applied them himself.

Strength and dynamic movement are at the root of successful jumping and throwing. Upper body development, arm movements and proper breathing are all essential in the field events.

Success depends on the athlete developing his own strengths. Each athlete's style should be a reflection of his personality, not of the accepted techniques of the day. The successful field event athletes, such as Al Oerter and Dick Fosbury, have been the ones who have differed from the norm and used their own individual style.

"To achieve the world records of the future," Cerutty said, "the athlete will have to invent some new techniques that are a reflection of his personality. Free expression is the only key that will open the door to the athlete's true potential."

Much of this individuality is destroyed when athletes blindly accept the orthodox methods.

"Weightmen, and not the jumpers as a rule place an over-emphasis on weight lifting to acquire brute strength in place of power," Percy said, "and any added bulk impairs the athlete's reflexes. This inhibits a total outpour of the personality by slowing down the delivery."

Like runners, field event athletes all tend to adopt the orthodox "zombie" movements. Things such as pulleys, muscle stretching devices and weight machines all encourage this. Strengthening should come primarily from the basic weight training exercises.

Jumpers are the athletes most in need of tensile strength. This can be achieved through gymnastics and intensive weight lifting. Many mistakenly train with extensive weight lifting, and this only builds unneeded bulky muscle.

THE THROWING EVENTS

The throwing events are largely trunk events, in which the athlete's hips, torso, shoulders and arms play a major role in generating the power for the throw. Proper breathing is very important in all of the throwing events. The athlete should inhale fully, hold the air in his lungs momentarily as he winds up for the throw, then audibly exhale it as the object is released.

All throwers need to do a great deal of work with weights. But strength does not necessarily show up in bulk. This is a misconception many throwers have.

"Added weight on a thrower only slows him down," Percy said. "Lifting heavy weights extensively does this. It impairs the reflexes. All throwers should develop strength by lifting weights with the intensive method."

All throwers should use the five basic lifting exercises along with these additional power lifts: clean and jerk, military press, high pulls and half-squats. The dead lift with twice the athlete's body weight is especially valuable. Some of the top hammer throwers, such as Gyula Zsivotzky, Uwe Beyer and Harold Connolly did dead lifts with 600 pounds.

After each lifting session, the athlete should hang limp on a horizontal bar to prevent shortening of the muscle fibers and to relax the muscles.

The shot put. The shot putter should divide his

Ludvik Danek, 1972 Olympic champion, displays his classic discus form.

training into building strength during the conditioning period, and neural pattern development in the practice period.

By the time the competitive season is underway, the shot putter should have developed the neural patterns so that most of his throws seem almost effortless.

Brian Oldfield, who broke the world record by more than a foot when he threw 72' 6 1/2," commented afterward, "I tell you, it felt effortless. I was on the wall of the circle before it hit, and I knew it was great."

To reach this state where it seems effortless involves a lot of effort in practice. Besides weight training, the shot putter should practice with overweight shots of 18, 20 or 25 pounds in the conditioning period. Very little putting with the regulation 16-pound shot should occur in this period. The intent of the conditioning period is to build strength through intensive lifting and putting with overweight shots.

When he is practicing, Cerutty believed the thrower should always keep his seasonal goal marked on the throwing field. Of course, he will never reach it with an overweight shot, but if it is always in sight, it will become imprinted in the shot putter's mind.

Other exercises that should occur in the conditioning period are wind sprints and running in place. These improve the athlete's speed and reflexes.

The shot putter should develop a wider range of movements. The traditional movement doesn't develop enough momentum. Brian Oldfield is the one athlete who has made progress in this respect. He goes through a wide range of movements in the circle before he releases the shot in a three-quarter turn, almost as in discus throwing. This enables him more leverage and momentum for his throw.

The development of tensile strength that is necessary in order to reach one's potential can be acquired in three ways during the conditioning period: (1) intensive weight lifting; (2) gymnastics; (3) running on the spot regularly at the end of a workout to speed up the thrower's reflexes.

Once the competition period begins, much of this strengthening work should taper down, as the shot putter begins to work on technique. The proper style should be stressed constantly in the latter part of the throwing-practice period and early part of the competition period, so that it will be permanently ingrained in the athlete's brain. He shouldn't have to be worrying about it during the important late season.

At first, the athlete should concentrate on a mark two feet short of the edge of the circle, as he practices throwing. The shot should be thrown at a 45-degree angle. It is helpful to watch films of this to learn the proper technique for releasing the shot.

In the competition period, he should throw the 16-pound shot to work on the fine points of his technique. With the strength and fast reflexes that built in during the other two periods, the thrower should reach his potential.

"The shot putter should practice using different

weights," Percy said, "both less than and greater than the regulation weight. When the competition occurs, he will throw farther than the athlete who has been training all along with the regulation weight."

The discus throw. The discus event is very similar to shot putting, both in training and in execution. One primary difference is a faster release in the slinging motion for the discus. Percy compares this with the uncoiling of a spring.

"The discus is held under tension as the thrower prepares," Percy said. "Then, he begins to uncoil like a spring to release the tension from his legs, hips, arms and chest."

Al Oerter, gold medalist in four consecutive Olympics from 1956-1968, has one of the best uncoiling motions, with a unique knee bend at the beginning of his approach that gives him added momentum during his delivery.

Like the shot put, the discus should be thrown at a 45-degree angle, with a three-quarter turn. Training for the event is similar to training for the shot put.

Gyula Zsivotsky, 1968 Olympic hammer champion, throws with free-flowing techniques.

Hammer throw. The hammer throw differs from the previous two throwing events in that the thrower makes four full turns before release, rather than just a single three-quarter turn. It is not advisable for an athlete to specialize in both the hammer throw and either the discus or the shot, since they involve conflicting neural patterns.

It is important to develop speed with an overweight hammer in the conditioning period. Generally speaking, the taller person has an advantage in this event since he has more leverage in his approach and a wider radius in each of his turns. However, fast reflexes are extremely important in this event, and if the thrower has excess bulk he will not have this explosive power. As in all track and field events, the thrower should strive to build tensile strength through intensive lifting.

Intensive weight training should dominate the conditioning period. In the throwing-practice period, the athlete should build the neural pattern that is smooth and effortless as he hovers down the circle to execute the four turns. The four turns in the hammer flow together like the four laps in a mile race.

The javelin. The javelin is a unique event. Throwers range in size from Finland's stocky Jorma Kinnunen to the tall, almost lanky throwers such as Janis Lusis of the Soviet Union and Bill Schmidt of the United States. There are also distinct differences in the Finnish, Russian and American styles of throwing the javelin. The release angle for the javelin can be anywhere from 30-45 degrees.

It is essential in top level javelin throwing that the thrower develops a very fast speed in the run up to the toe board. He should practice some hill running running in place during the conditioning period.

Full-lung aeration is important in this event. When the athlete makes his approach, he should hold in the air just before the release of the javelin and then expel it vocally when he throws.

The athlete who is naturally suited for the javelin

should be able to throw a softball farther than an athlete in any other event. During a visit with famous Austrian coach Franz Stampfl, he told me, "The best javelin throwers in the world can pick up a softball and throw it out of sight. That's how strong the javelin thrower has to be if he expects to throw the javelin 300 feet."

TRAINING FOR THE THROWING EVENTS

Training for each one of the throwing events is similar. Differences have been noted in the individual discussions of each event. As in all events, the training program should be divided into a six-month conditioning period and a three-month throwing-practice period.

Sample weeks in each of the two periods follow:

CONDITIONING PERIOD

Mornings

Two or three days per week, the athlete should run 2-3 miles at a varied pace.

Afternoons

Monday: 2 hours of intensive weight lifting, with the five basic lifts and several power lifts.
Hang limp on the horizontal bar.
Play catch with a 50-pound medicine ball for 15-30 minutes.
Run on the spot for five minutes.

Tuesday: An hour of gymnastics, including work on the roman rings, parallel bars and vaulting horse, and ending with chin-ups.
Practice throwing an overweight implement for 30 minutes.
Run in place for five minutes or play a fast moving sport such as basketball or football for 30 minutes.

Wednesday: Two hours of intensive weight lifting.
Hang limp on the horizontal bar.
Throw an overweight implement for 30 minutes.

Thursday: An hour of gymnastics.
100- and 220-yard sprints at full speed.
Jog and rest.
Run on the spot for five minutes.

Friday: Throw an overweight implement for an hour.
Catch a 50-pound medicine ball for a half-hour.
Run in place for five minutes.

Saturday: 2 hours of intensive weight lifting.
Run in place for five minutes.

Sunday: Rest.

THROWING-PRACTICE PERIOD

Mornings

For the first half of this period, there should be at least one cross-country run per week of 2-3 miles at a varied pace. This should taper down and then stop entirely in the final weeks of competition.

AFTERNOON

Monday: One hour of intensive weight lifting.
Practice approach movement with an underweight implement for 30 minutes.

Tuesday: 30 minutes of gymnastics.
Throw a 50-pound medicine ball for 20 minutes.
Run in place for seven minutes.

Wednesday: Throw an overweight implement for 30 minutes.
Practice approach.
One hour of intensive weight lifting.
Run in place for five minutes.

Thursday: Throw an underweight implement for 30-45 minutes.
Run 80-yard sprints full speed.
Run in place for seven minutes.

Friday: Catch the medicine ball for 20 minutes.

Saturday: Competition.

Sunday: Rest.

In the conditioning period, heavy weight lifting should be done three days a week for up to 2 1/2 hours per session. On the non-lifting days, the thrower should practice with an overweight implement, do gymnastics and/or catch a 50-pound medicine ball. Chin-ups and work on the Roman rings are good supplementary exercises, as is trampoline jumping and work on the vaulting horse. In the conditioning period, it is good practice to end each workout with several minutes of running in place at a varied but quick rate. Some cross-country running of 2-3 miles is also advisable in the conditioning period.

In the throwing-practice period, the athlete should begin sharpening his throwing by practicing with a lighter throwing weight and tapering down the endurance training to work on technique.

THE JUMPING EVENTS

More than any other track and field events, the

jumping events demand a great deal of spring in the legs. This comes primarily from the tensile strength that is gained through intensive weight lifting. Gymnastics also are valuable in the development of this.

Proper breathing, speed and coordination are all essential and thus require a variety of training to develop.

The athlete must develop a neural pattern that lets him *believe* he can jump a certain height. Percy would tell the jumpers, "The trampoline is a valuable aid to the jumper because it puts back the spring in the achilles tendons that is lost by pounding the hard runways. When bouncing on the "tramp" the athlete should picture himself jumping over a new height. Then, he should practice hard to achieve his goal. Eventually, the mind and body catch up with reality. The jumper should never place limitations on himself!"

"When the jumper goes for the world record in his event," Percy said, "he must concentrate on the new height or distance and project his mind and body beyond the barrier."

The long jump. All of the great long jumpers possess tremendous speed over 100 yards. The more speed the jumper can generate in his approach, the faster he will be able to propel himself in the jump. The jumper should lift himself completely off the ground and concentrate on landing on a certain spot. He should inhale oxygen as he hits the take-off board, then exhale as he is in the midst of his jump.

It is important during the conditioning period, and particularly in the jumping practice period that the long jumper conditions a fast approach run. His steps to the take-off board should be instinctive without any check marks in the competitive period because he has already formed the proper neural pattern.

The conditioning period should be spent doing some distance running, windsprints, intensive weight lifting, gymnastics and running on the spot.

The triple jump. The triple jump is similar to the long jump, except there are two additional jumping movements.

Rhythm is very important in this event. The jumper should develop speed in his approach, build this momentum with the first two motions, and then make the final move, which is simply a long jump.

Attaining this rhythm involves practicing the jump and developing upper body strength. As in the long jump, the triple jumper should inhale as he leaves the ground, exhale as he is in the air, inhale a second time on the step and inhale on the final jump.

The high jump. There have been a number of radically different, though all successful high jump styles over the years, from the straddle jump popularized by John Thomas to the Russian style of straddling to the roll to the Fosbury "flop."

Cerutty believed these were all aiming for the most efficient jumping style which, when achieved, would resemble the way a horse jumps over a barrier.

"I teach the jumpers at Portsea to run up to the bar at a 90-degree angle and jump over the bar like a horse does in the equestrian events," Cerutty said. "In this technique, the jumper runs to the bar and dives up into the air with his arms going over first like the forelegs of a horse."

The angle of approach to the bar is something that differs greatly. In the Russian "Dyatchkov straddle," the jumper approaches the bar at an angle of 20-28 degrees. In the Fosbury style, the angle is 40 degrees.

The pole vault. The pole vault is nothing more than a "hand stand" in mid-air. All top vaulters seem to possess gymnastics skills, and both gymnastics and hand stands should be a part of the practice. The vaulter can practice hand stands by hanging onto a rope and twisting his body straight up into the air like he is vaulting.

In the jumping-practice period, the vaulter should practice over a lower height to develop confidence in his style. He should not aim for specific heights until

CONDITIONING PERIOD

Mornings

Fartlek 3-5 miles twice a week.

Afternoons

Monday: An hour of gymnastics, including work on the roman rings, rope-climbing, chin-ups and work on the vaulting horse.
Run on the spot for 10-15 minutes at a fast, varied pace.

Tuesday: An hour and a half of intensive weight lifting.
Play a fast moving sport for 30-45 minutes.
Run on the spot for 10 minutes.

Wednesday: Uphill springs for an hour.
Run in place for 10-15 minutes.

Thursday: Two hours of intensive weight lifting.
Run on the spot for 5-7 minutes.

Friday: One hour of gymnastics.
100- and 220-yard sprints all-out.

Saturday: One and one-half hours of intensive weight lifting.
Practice technique/rhythm for 30 minutes.
Run on the spot for 10 minutes.

Sunday: Rest.

JUMPING-PRACTICE PERIOD

Mornings

Three miles in the morning once or twice a week until mid-season.

Afternoons

Monday: One hour of gymnastics.
Thirty minutes of jumping.
Run on the spot for 10 minutes.
Tuesday: Practice technique for 1-2 hours.
Windsprints.
45 minutes of intensive weight lifting.

Wednesday: Sprint up a steep hill for 30 minutes.
Practice jumping for 45 minutes.
Run in place for 5-7 minutes.

Thursday: An hour of intensive weight lifting.
Wind sprints for 10 minutes.
Jumping.

Friday: Practice jumps for 20 minutes.

Saturday: Competition.

Sunday: Rest.

the final months of the competitive season. Most of the conditioning period is spent lifting weights and doing free-form gymnastics.

The trampoline will be an important part of the vaulter's routine as he will do a lot of sommersaults high in the air to improve his spatial judgment for scaling great heights over 18 feet.

TRAINING FOR THE JUMPING EVENTS

All of the jumping events are similar. Individual differences are noted in each section.

There seems to be a large split between the track events and the field events. The field events seem alien to many running event athletes, and vice versa. But the theories of natural movement and full-lung aeration apply equally to both.

"Regardless of what event it is," Cerutty said, "whether high jumping or running the marathon, when the athlete understands the proper way to move and fill his lungs, there will be new records in *every* event."

12

Decathlon and Pentathlon

The decathlon is possibly the most difficult event in track and field. It is a two-day event in which the athlete competes in the 100 meters, long jump, shot put, high jump, 400 meters (first day), 110-meter hurdles, discus throw, pole vault, javelin throw and the 1500 meters (second day).

The hardest, most challenging aspect of the decathlon is conditioning the body to register the 10 neural patterns so the athlete will excel on the highest creative plane.

Percy Cerutty believed most decathlon athletes were underdeveloped in their lung usage. He thought that their 1500-meter times were inferior to their performances in the other events, and this was because they did not develop the lung power necessary for good middle-distance running. If they did this, he believed they would perform better not only in the 1500 meters, but in all of the other events as well.

"In my observations of Milt Campbell, Rafer Johnson and Yang Chuan-Kwang," Percy said, "I found that top decathlon athletes were naturally best in the 110-meter hurdles, 400 meters and pole vault. One of the biggest disappointments in the decathlon is that the athlete can run the 400 meters under 50 seconds, but can't put four 60 second quarters together to run at four-minute mile pace. When the athlete strengthens his cardiovascular system by lifting heavy weights, running up sand hills and learning to fill his lungs, he should be able to improve in all the events and still have the strength to run a 3:43 1500, which is a four-minute mile pace."

In the Olympics, the United States has dominated this event with such champions as Jim Thorpe (1912), Harold Osborn (1924), Glenn Morris (1936), Bob Mathias (1948, 1952), Milt Campbell (1956), Rafer Johnson (1960), Bill Toomey (1968) and Bruce Jenner (1976).

TRAINING FOR THE DECATHLON

Cerutty believed that the decathlon demands a more complex training program than any other event, since the athlete has to condition himself for 10 separate events.

"The decathlon athlete must first develop basic strength and endurance," he said, "then he should work on the techniques and strengths necessary for all 10 individual events."

Building large amounts of strength, agility and endurance is the key to success in the decathlon. It is not efficient just to practice the 10 events. There should also be distance running, gymnastics, hill running and weight lifting.

"The athlete should not waste his time trying to excel in the events in practice," Percy said. "This just frustrates most athletes, because they aren't ready for any technique work until they've first built a base for it. This can be done through such activities as swimming, weight lifting, distance running and cross-country skiing."

The most important aspect in training for the decathlon is first building this endurance base, mostly through non-event training, then conditioning the 10 neural patterns in the decathlon-practice period.

The conditioning period. In this period, the athlete should run 40-50 miles per week. This should be done by varied-pace cross-country running each morning, and then one long run per week of 10-15 miles. Since he is doing this much running, the decathlete might want to run some cross-country events.

Three afternoons per week should be devoted primarily to weight lifting. These sessions should last for 1-2 hours each. Besides the five basic lifts, there should be some additional power lifting.

The only individual event training that the athlete should do is practice throwing an overweight discus, shot or javelin.

Two days each week the afternoon session should center around gymnastics. Exercises should include rope-climbing, chin-ups and trampoline and Roman ring work.

Other strength building workouts should include uphill running and wind sprints in the sand.

A sample week midway through the conditioning period follows:

Mornings

Fartlek 3-5 miles over varied terrain.

Afternoons

Monday: 1½ hours of intensive weight lifting with the basic lifts and several supplementary power lifts.
Hang limp on the horizontal bar for two minutes.
Play catch with a 50-pound medicine ball.
Run in place for 10-12 minutes.

Tuesday: An hour of gymnastics.
Sprint up a steep hill for 30-45 minutes.
Run in place for 10-12 minutes.

Wednesday: 1½ hours of intensive weight lifting.
Hang limp on the horizontal bar for two minutes.
Play catch with a 50-pound medicine ball.
Run in place for 10-12 minutes.

Thursday: Thirty to 45 minutes of wind sprints in sand.
Practice throwing an overweight implement for an hour.
Run in place for 10-12 minutes.

Friday: 1½ hours of intensive weight lifting.
Hang limp on the horizontal bar for two minutes.
Play catch with a 50-pound medicine ball.
Run in place for 10-12 minutes.

Saturday: 12-mile run at a varied pace.

Sunday: Rest.

The progression of training in the six-month conditioning period is very important. The volume of work should steadily increase, until the midway mark (three months). Then, the athlete should concentrate more on intensity. He should not try to run farther; he should try to run faster.

The six months of the conditioning period are spent working to build cardio-vascular strength. The athlete then has the proper base to start the conditioning process for each individual event in the decathlon-practice period.

"Training hard and thoroughly in the weeks before a decathlon event means almost nothing if the athlete doesn't have the proper endurance base," Cerutty said.

Taking one's pulse rate periodically during this period is a good gauge of how well this endurance base is being developed.

The decathlon-practice period. Developing the 10 neural patterns in the athlete's mind is the main goal during this period. He should begin working on the individual events so that they flow together. If some events are much more developed than others, the athlete will not have this flow and will have trouble once the competition is underway.

Each one of the 10 events in the decathlon must be practiced with balance so that the athlete will not upset the total flow and natural rhythm of his neural patterns. He should never overcompensate in his training by working on his weaker events and neglecting his strong events. This will ruin the overall flow and rhythm for the 10 events and cause inconsistent scores. The best way for the athlete to develop a strong active neural pattern for the decathlon is by blending each one of the 10 neural patterns together.

In the 100 meters, the runner should practice one-third segments of the race as well as starting out of the blocks. He should practice exhaling as he leaves the blocks, then taking a single breath in each one-third segment.

In the hurdles, he should especially work on his steps between each hurdle, and make sure he has the same lead leg and arm going over the barrier.

Segment running should be practiced for the 400- and 1500-meter runs.

The athlete should also practice his jumping approach and technique, and work with overweight implements.

A sample week midway through the decathlon-practice period follows:

Monday
Morning: Practice segments and starts for the 100-yard dash.
Practice long jumping.
Run in place for five minutes.
Afternoon: 30-45 minutes of running at a varied pace with several all-out surges.
Practice throwing an overweight shot put for 30-45 minutes.
Run in place for 5-10 minutes.

Tuesday
Morning: 30-45 minutes of high jump approach and jumping technique.
30 minutes of wind sprints.
Afternoon: 30-45 minutes of segment running for the 400 meters on a grass track.
Fartlek, 2-5 miles.

Wednesday
Morning: Two miles at a varied pace.
30-45 minutes of hurdle practice and discus throw.
Afternoon: 30-45 minutes of gymnastics.
Run in place for 10 minutes.

Thursday
Morning: 30-45 minutes of pole vault approach and jumping technique.
30-45 minutes of wind sprints.
Afternoon: 30-45 minutes of throwing with an overweight javelin.
Run in place for 10-15 minutes.

Friday
Morning: Surges of 330, 440, 660 and 1½ miles for 45-60 minutes.
Afternoon: 30-45 minutes of technique practice in several events.
Play catch with a 50-pound medicine ball.

Saturday
Afternoon: Perform all 10 events.

Sunday
Rest.

The decathlon-practice period should start with the athlete practicing several events each day *in the order they come in competition.* At first, he should just concentrate on technique, then add rhythm. But as the period progresses, he should increase the stress he applies practicing each event, gradually cutting down the quantity as he increases the quality of his workouts.

During the week, the athlete can practice the 10 events over a period of several days if the proper sequence is not interrupted. This will reinforce the 10 neural patterns so that in the competitive situation they will be done in one smooth flowing performance.

On the weekends, the athlete should practice all of the events in a time trial to develop the necessary flow. This should be done on Friday and Saturday to prepare the athlete for the two days of competition.

If the decathlete is competing in a track meet on the weekend, he could do four events from the first or second day of competition and finish the meet with a run over 400 meters or a mile (1500 meters).

Competition. Once the regular, important competition is underway, overall training volume should be cut back sharply. The emphasis should be on sharpening with short intense workouts.

By this time, the flowing together of the 10 events should be natural. The athlete should not be overly worried or confident about any single one, but should mentally prepare for the next event as he completes each one to the best of his ability. Because of the nature of this event, the athlete must concentrate specifically on his own performance in the individual events.

"The decathlon athlete who is destined to be an Olympic champion must learn to be indifferent to the other athletes while he is competing in all 10 events," Cerutty said. "This type of a competitive attitude doesn't mean that the performer should mentally block out the other competitors altogether, but it is more important that he concentrate on his techniques rather than on trying to beat the other opponents. The athlete will find that he can total a higher score in the decathlon if he concentrates on all of the 10 events in a broad spectrum, even though he is only competing in one event at a time.

"As an example, the decathlete would be dashing down the track in the 100 meters and during this event he would start the wheels turning in his mind for the long jump and shot put which come next. This is a similar principle to that in a game of billiards, where the player concentrates on a series of shots while he is actually making one shot on the table so that he can move on to the other shots that he has planned in his mind. Each shot leads to the next. The decathlon is similar because the person has to generate a lot of energy and momentum that will carry him through all of the events during the two days of competition."

A sample week in the serious competitive season follows:

Monday

Afternoon: 1½ hours of 100-meter, long jump and shot put practice.

Tuesday

Morning: 1½ hours of high jump, 110-meter hurdles and discus throw practice.

Afternoon: 30-45 minutes of varied pace running, including 330, 440 and 660 surges.

Wednesday

Afternoon: 1½ hours of pole vault and javelin throw practice.

Run in place for 10-15 minutes.

Thursday

Rest for competition.

Friday

Competition.

Saturday

Competition.

Sunday

Rest.

There are several differences between Percy Cerutty's ideas about the decathlon and the standard ideas. The most basic one is that the athlete needs a six-month endurance-building period in which there is almost no practice of the specific event, but a great deal of general conditioning.

The purpose of this general conditioning period is to develop the proper body movements and breathing patterns to perform well in all of the 10 decathlon events.

"Higher scores in the decathlon will come from new techniques, better training programs, faster reflexes and full lung aeration," Percy said. "This need for oxygen applies to all of the events, not just the running ones."

WOMEN'S PENTATHLON

The women's pentathlon in the Olympic Games is the ultimate test of the female's speed, strength, stamina and her level of endurance.

In 1964 at the Tokyo Olympic Games, the pentathlon was added to the program of events. In the 1968 Olympic Games at Mexico City, the distance for the 80-meter hurdles was lengthened to a 100 meters. After the 1976 Olympic Games, the 200 meters was replaced by the 800 meters so the pentathlon would be an all-around test for the female athlete.

The pentathlon has been dominated by the women from Europe with victories from Irina Press of the Soviet Union in 1964, Ingred Becker of West Germany in 1968, Mary Peters from Great Britain in 1972, and in the Montreal Games of 1976, there was a tie for the gold medal between Siegrun Siegl and Cristine Laser of East Germany. Siegrun Siegl was declared the winner because she won three out of the five events.

The woman who is naturally gifted with a tall and slender build is the ideal type of an athlete for the pentathlon. With the addition of the 800 meters, the endurance factor is extremely important.

The 100-meter hurdles, 400 meters and high jump are the three events that have become the major stepping stones to greatness in the pentathlon. The classic example is Irina Press of the Soviet Union who won the 80-meter hurdles at the Rome Games in 1960, and then went on to win the gold medal in the pentathlon at the 1964 Olympic Games.

The training year for the pentathlon should be divided into the conditioning period (six months), the pentathlon practice period (three months), and the competition period, which extends over the last three months of the season.

The women in the pentathlon should approach their training year with basically the same type of conditioning program that the men follow in the decathlon. The women, like the men in the decathlon, should follow an intensive program of training with a high quality of weight lifting. The pentathlete will lift the heaviest weights that are possible for her in short sets of 2-3 repetitions. This type of weight training develops tensile strength.

The pentathlete should do some distance running during the conditioning period to strengthen her cardio-vascular system for the 800 meters, and also for the long hours that she will be competing during the two days of the intense competition. The distance running in the morning will relax the woman's mind and body, and at the same time it will work as a balance in her training program to offset the stress from the power workouts.

The conditioning period (six months). During the conditioning period, the pentathlete should cover approximately 10-15 miles each week by running 2-3 miles every morning before breakfast. When the woman is running each day, she will try to develop a rhythmic stride pattern by trotting, cantering and galloping over a variety of undulating terrain.

"Every two or three weeks, the pentathlete should compete in a cross-country meet," Percy said. "The times over these distances are very important because they can be used as an accurate measuring rod so the athlete and her coach can regulate the intensity of her daily workouts each week as the conditioning period rapidly draws to a close. By the end of the six months, the woman's basic pulse rate should be down in the neighborhood of 40-45 beats per minute. The women can add a little variation to their training programs by doing some long- distance swimming at a relaxed pace in the morning for about an hour and a half if the weather is too cold outside."

A sample week in the conditioning period follows:

Mornings

Fartlek 2-3 miles by trotting, cantering, and galloping over beach, park or on the golf course. Rest and recover.

Afternoons

Monday: An hour and a half of lifting weights.
Hang limp on the horizontal bar for about three minutes.
Rest shortly.
Practice with 10 and 12 pound shots for 20 minutes.
Rest shortly.
Play catch with a 14-pound medicine ball, and then go out to the track, and do some windsprints over one of the following distances: 220, 330, 440 or 660 yards. Surge on the spot for 5-6 minutes.

Tuesday: An hour of gymnastics by climbing the ropes, 'skinning the cat' on the roman rings, chin-ups on the horizontal bar, jumping high on the trampoline to strengthen the athlete's natural spring in her legs and working on the parallel bars and the vaulting horse.
Rest shortly.
Sprint up a steep hill with a grade of 1-2 for about 20 minutes.
Rest and recover.
Run on the spot for 5 minutes.
Arm raisers.

Wednesday: Repeat Monday's workout.
On this day, go out to the track, golf course, or the park and do some windsprints over 440 yards.

Thursday: Repeat Tuesday's workout.

Friday: Repeat Monday's workout.
On this day, go out to the track, golf course, or the park and do some windsprints over 660 yards.

Saturday: No morning workout.
In the afternoon, the pentathlete can go on a 10-mile hike in the mountains with a 10-pound pack on her back, or she can play a fast moving sport like tennis, handball, soccer, golf, or basketball.
Every two or three weeks, she will compete in a cross-country meet.

Sunday: Rest and recovery for the next week of work.

During the three months, the pentathlete should plan her training schedules so that she will accomplish two things. First, she should retain the high level of conditioning that was established in the first six months. Secondly, she should be balancing each one of the five events together so that she will have a strong active neural pattern for the competition period.

The pentathlete should divide her practice period into three five-week periods like the men do in the decathlon, so that she can gradually condition her mind and body for the five events.

These are sample workouts for the three month pentathlon-practice period:

First Five Weeks

Mornings

Monday-Wednesday: Weight lifting for about an hour
Surge uphill or gymnastics.
Run on the spot for 5-6 minutes.
Arm raisers.

Afternoons

Monday: Run through a series of 100-meter hurdles for about 45 minutes.
Rest shortly.
Run some windsprints on the track over 660 yards for about 15 minutes.
Rest shortly.
Run on the spot for 5-6 minutes.
Arm raisers.

Tuesday: Practice the long jump for about 45 minutes.
Rest shortly.
Go to the park and run some windsprints over 440 yards for about 15 minutes.
Rest shortly.
Run on the spot for 5-6 minutes.
Arm raisers.

Wednesday: To add some variation to the athlete's training program, she can play a fast moving sport like tennis, handball, soccer, golf or basketball.

Thursday: Rest for the time trial on Friday and Saturday.

Friday: Time trial in the 100-meter hurdles.

Saturday: Time trial in the long jump.

Sunday: Rest and recovery for the next week of work.

Second Five Weeks

Mornings

Monday-Wednesday: Gymnastics for an hour.
Weight lifting or distance running.

Afternoons

Monday: Practice the 100-meter hurdles and the shot put (six and seven pounds) for an hour and a half.
Rest shortly.
Run some windsprints on the track over 330 yards for about 10 minutes.
Rest shortly.
Run on the spot for 5-6 minutes. Arm raisers.

Tuesday: Practice the long jump and the 800 meters. The runner should practice her breathing rhythms while she is blending the different sections of her race together.
Rest shortly.
Arm raisers.
Shower.

Wednesday: To add some variation to the athlete's training program, she can play a fast moving sport like tennis, handball, soccer, golf or basketball.

Thursday: Rest for the time trials on Friday and Saturday.

Friday: Time trial in the 100-meter hurdles and the shot put.

Saturday: Time trial in the long jump and the 800 meters.

Sunday: Rest and recover for the next week of work.

Third Five Weeks

Mornings

Monday-Thursday: Surge up a steep hill, weight lifting or gymnastics.
Rest shortly.
Run on the spot for 5-6 minutes.
Arm raisers.

Afternoons

Monday: Practice the 100 meter hurdles, shot put (six and seven pounds), and the high jump for two hours.
Rest shortly.
Run some windsprints on the track over 330 yards for about 10 minutes.
Rest shortly to recover your wind and strength.
Run on the spot for 5-6 minutes.
Arm raisers.

Tuesday: Practice the long jump and the 800 meters. In the 800 meters, the runner will still continue to surge over the following distances of

(continued from page 147)

220, 330, 440 and 660 yards with the times that will be done on the track during the competition period.
Rest shortly.
Run on the spot for 5-6 minutes.
Arm raisers.

Wednesday: To add some variation to the athlete's training program, she can play a fast moving sport like tennis, handball, soccer, golf or basketball.

Thursday: Work on starts out of the blocks for 30 minutes.
Run on the spot for 5-6 minutes.
Shower.

Friday: Rest for the time trial on Saturday.

Saturday: Time trial over the five events in the pentathlon.
Compare the marks with the other time trials.

Sunday: Rest and recovery for the next week of work.

The competition period (3 months)

Mornings

Monday-Wednesday: Gymnastics, weight lifting or uphill sprints.

Afternoons

Monday: Practice the 100-meter hurdles and the shot put for an hour.
Rest shortly.
Run some windsprints on the track over 110 yards for about 10 minutes.
Rest shortly.
Run on the spot for 5-6 minutes.
Arm raisers.

Tuesday: Practice the high jump for 45 minutes.
Rest shortly.
Go to the park and run some windsprints over 220 yards for about 10 minutes.
Rest shortly.
Run on the spot for 5-6 minutes.
Arm raisers.

Wednesday: Practice the long jump for 45 minutes.
Rest shortly.
Go to the park and run some windsprints over 330 yards for about 10 minutes.
Rest shortly.
Run on the spot for 5-6 minutes.
Arm raisers.

Thursday: Rest and meditation for the first day of competition on Friday.

Friday: Competition

Saturday: Competition

Sunday: Rest

13

Race Walking

Walking had a great impact on the restoration of Percy Cerutty's life after his near-fatal physical and mental collapse in 1938. As he began his program of natural diet, weight lifting, swimming and running, he also took long hikes through the Australian wilderness.

It was that same year that he founded the Melbourne Walking Club. This was not for serious competitive runners; it was for a small group of fitness enthusiasts who enjoyed hiking and mountaineering. Percy was the "pied piper" of the group, which went on regular long excursions, sometimes as far as 50 miles. To keep everyone's spirits up, he would play his harmonica and recite his prose and poetry.

Walking also played a large role in the formulation of Cerutty's five basic movements. During his trek up Mount Kosciusko, he found that using the galloping method, interspersed with walking, he could travel up the mountain quicker than a fast-moving pack of mules.

This is how Cerutty developed the basic movements. During his long hikes, he would walk for a while, then break into a canter and a gallop. He let his instincts dictate which of the basic movements to adopt. At Portsea, he encouraged his athletes to go off on long, solitary hikes, so they could practice the rotation of the basic movements and learn more about themselves at the same time.

Self-knowledge is gained by this solitary practice. When the runner goes off on an even-paced run, his thinking tends to become very uniform. But when he alternates movements and does some walking, his thinking becomes more varied. Percy developed the ideas and many of the actual lines for his poetry in lengthy walk-runs along the beach. He advocated that all distance runners train at a varied pace which sometimes slowed to a walk.

RACE WALKING

Race walking is one of the more neglected events in athletics. Many potentially great race walkers never take up the sport because they cannot give it 100% dedication.

"True greatness is never achieved noisily," Percy said. This can be applied to almost anything, but when Cerutty said it, he was referring to race walking.

Cerutty himself race walked before his concentration shifted specifically to distance running.

As in running, the area most in need of development in walking is full lung usage. Noel Freeman, silver medalist in the 1960 Olympic 20-kilometer walk, was the athlete who best utilized Cerutty's ideas.

The abdominal muscles are especially important in proper striding for the walking events, so sit-ups and hill running should play a large role in the conditioning period. If the abdominals are properly developed, the walker can lengthen his stride and have a lighter foot plant.

"As with the long running events, the walker should land with a noiseless 'slithering' footfall," Percy said. "He should not plod along with a noisy thump."

The edge of the foot should land first. If this is not happening, the walker should work on it during the conditioning period. Cerutty was opposed to the popular style in which the heel hits first, then the ball of the foot.

The essential breathing technique is acquired only by first developing the proper arm movements and strengthening the upper body with the basic weight lifting exercises.

"The runner and the race walker both move on upper-body strength that is transferred to the legs through full, proper oxygen consumption," Percy said. "To fully fill his lungs, the walker cannot move with locked elbows. This immobilizes his oxygen consumption. He should lift his shoulders up high as he inhales. When he exhales, he should throw his arms to his side. The fingers should be pinched together on inhalation and then opened up on exhalation.

"The toes should be pointed slightly inward as the race walker moves. In a relaxed stride that is smooth and flowing, the walker's knees should 'kiss' each other. The race walker, like the distance runner, can only develop full strength when his movements are relaxed. The athlete should never have to force the flow of his pace, as this will abnormally lengthen his stride and in the process cause stress and strain on the entire musculature.

"When the athlete's abdominal muscles are strengthened from running on sand hills and doing sit-ups on the incline board, the stride can be lengthened naturally. My experiments here at Portsea with hundreds of athletes have proven to me that calisthenics, mobility exercises and high knee-lifts are useless in lengthening one's stride. All this does is ruin the flow of his movement. The race walker should have flowing movements like a ballet dancer."

Race walkers usually improve with age. Veteran walkers such as Larry Young, Bernd Kannenberg, Todd Scully, Ron Laird and Vladimir Golubnichiy have all steadily improved as they've matured. Golubnichiy won medals in the Olympic Games from 1960-1972.

Many distance runners turn to walking late in their career. Some who are only good runners find that they are very good walkers.

TRAINING

Training for the two basic walks, the 20-kilometer and the 50-kilometer, will obviously be quite different, since the latter is 2 1/2 times longer than the former. Training for the 50-kilometer should involve much more endurance work, particularly in the conditioning period. Typical endurance workouts are a 30-mile walk with a 40-pound pack on the walker's back and cross-country skiing.

The 20-kilometer walker also should stress endurance in the conditioning period, but should include some faster walking and less overall volume.

Weight lifting should be done by walkers in both events, using the intensive method and the five basic exercises.

Most of the running-walking practice should be on sand, grass or dirt. Once a week, to better strengthen the tendons in the legs and feet, the walker should train barefoot in sand or grass.

The conditioning period. Strength building and proper breathing technique are the important areas to work on in the conditioning period.

Using the proper body movements enhances full breathing and lets the walker glide over the ground without ever breaking contact.

The 50-K walker should average 10-15 miles per day in the second half of the conditioning period. The 20-K walker should average 8-10. This should come largely through varied-pace walk-runs at a fast overall rate. The athlete should let his instincts determine when he runs and when he walks.

"It is not the number of miles that is important," Percy said, "but the overall intensity. The walker should concentrate on a fast, but varied overall pace."

There should be some occasional long overdistance work. The 50-K walker, for instance, should try to work up to 35 miles in training and the 20-K walker up to 20. Long 50-mile hikes are also good to do once a month.

Occasionally, the resistance of a weighted vest or

heavy backpack should be used in this period.

After each workout, the walker should run in place at a fast rate. This is a speed building exercise and is equally valuable for the 20-K and the 50-K.

Gymnastics, hill training and weight lifting should all be practiced regularly in this period.

A sample week midway through the conditioning period follows:

Mornings

20-K: 3-8 miles at a varied pace.
50-K: 5-10 miles at a varied pace.

Afternoons

Monday: An hour of intensive weight lifting.
Hang limp on the horizontal bar for two minutes.
20-K: Five-mile walk at a varied pace.
Run in place for 10-15 minutes.
50-K: Eight-mile walk at a varied pace.
Run in place for 5-10 minutes.

Tuesday: An hour of gymnastics.
20-K: Three-mile walk-run at a varied pace.
Run in place for 10-15 minutes.
50-K: Seven-mile walk-run at a varied pace.
Run in place for 5-10 minutes.

Wednesday: An hour of intensive weight lifting.
Hang limp on the horizontal bar for two minutes.
20-K: 18-mile walk at a varied pace.
Run in place for 10-15 minutes.
50-K: 30-mile walk at a varied pace.
Run in place for 5-10 minutes.

Thursday: Six miles at a varied pace.
Run in place for 5-10 minutes.

Friday: *20-K:* Uphill sprints for 45 minutes.
Three-mile walk.
Run in place for 10-15 minutes.
50-K: Uphill sprints for 90 minutes.
Five-mile walk.
Run in place for 5-10 minutes.

Saturday: *20-K:* Walk and run eight miles.
Run in place for 10-15 minutes.
50-K: Walk and run 12 miles.
Run in place for 5-10 minutes.

Sunday: Rest.

The race-practice period. In this period, conditioning work should taper off, and the walker should begin doing faster spins including intervals.

The major emphasis of the early race-practice period is to build a proper neural pattern so that the walker learns to go the full distance at a determined pace. This is done by practicing the race in segments and then connecting them together.

In the second half of this period, the walker should have regular progress tests, in the form of a time trial or race.

If the walker feels overtaxed or mentally "stale" in this period, he should cut back on the volume of his training load, but should still get in several intensive workouts each week.

A sample week midway through the race-practice period follows:

Monday
20-K: Sprint up a steep hill for 30 minutes.
Walk seven miles at a fast, varied pace.
Run in place for 10-15 minutes.
50-K: Sprint up a steep hill for an hour.
Walk 12 miles at a fast, varied pace.
Run in place for 5-10 minutes.

Tuesday
20-K: 45 minutes of intensive weight lifting.
Hang limp on the horizontal bar for two minutes.
Walk four miles with a series of fast 880 intervals.
50-K: 45 minutes of intensive weight lifting.
Hang limp on the horizontal bar for two minutes.
Walk 10 miles with a series of fast one-mile intervals.

Thursday:
20-K: Eight miles at a varied pace.
Run in place for 10-15 minutes.
50-K: 16 miles at a varied pace.
Run in place for 5-10 minutes.

Firday
20-K: Two miles at a varied pace.
50-K: Six miles at a varied pace.

Saturday
Race or time trial.

Sunday
Rest.

Competition. When the serious competition is underway, the walker's program should be one of continual sharpening. Weight lifting and other supplemental exercises, which should taper down in the early part of the race-practice period, should cease entirely in the final weeks of competition.

There should still be one 10-15-mile stroll a week but it should be at a fast, varied pace. This should fall in the middle of the week if the walker is competing on weekends.

A sample week during the serious competitive season follows:

Monday

20-K: Walk six miles at a varied pace, including several all-out surges.

50-K: Walk 12 miles at a varied pace, including several all-out surges.

Tuesday

20-K: Uphill sprinting for 25 minutes.
Run in place for 10-15 minutes.

50-K: Uphill sprinting for 40 minutes.
Run in place for 5-10 minutes.

Wednesday

20-K: Two fast three-mile walks.

50-K: Three fast four-mile walks.

Thursday

20-K: Four miles of sprint walking.

50-K: Eight miles of sprint walking.

Friday

Run in place for 10-15 minutes.

Saturday

Competition.

Sunday

Rest

Much more than distance running, walking is an event that is far from its full development.

"Even with their varied motions, race walkers do not move their arms properly to allow for full-lung aeration," Cerutty said.

By raising their shoulders and using the basic movements, walkers will be able to flow through the walk at a much faster pace, moving almost noiselessly.

"The best athletes always grunted and fumed their way to the world records at the Olympic

Games!" Percy said. "The spectators in the stadium are not close enough to the action on the track to really appreciate the masterly efforts of a champion."

14

Recreational Running

The Greek and Roman Empires fell because of the moral and physical deterioration of the masses. The people lost touch with their bodies, and thus became slaves to the worldly possesions that were acquired from the countries they conquered. This led to high divorce rates, suicides, over-indulgence in exotic foods, extravagant debauchery of sex, luxurious living by depending on captured slaves and a corrupt government that misused public taxes.

Moralists believe the same thing could happen again in modern-day culture.

Percy Cerutty said, "Nature's laws can never be opposed by anyone."

The medical profession continues to invent new medicines to deal with physical ailments, but this wouldn't be necessary if people did something to stop the ailments before they occurred.

Cerutty didn't make many statements in favor of jogging. He was much more involved with competitive running. But he did believe everyone should exercise, and his theories of natural movement were applicable to everyone, not just top competitive runners.

"What is the use of 'killing yourself' all your life to make a million dollars, if you die before you can enjoy it?" he said. "Exercise is the best investment anyone can make in terms of his health and life expectancy."

Cerutty recommended that both the young and old should jog, lift weights, play tennis, swim, take walks. The important thing is to keep the body and mind exercised. You will find that keeping the body in shape does wonders for your mental attitude.

Physically, jogging increases the circulation of blood, which oxidizes the poisons in the body.

High cholesterol and hardening of the arteries are common problems people have today. There is much discussion about whether exercise can clear this up. Normal exercise does so only very slowly, because not enough oxygen gets to the bloodstream. But adopting Cerutty's principles of natural movement speeds up this process. Full-lung aeration speeds the oxygen consumption and the oxidation of toxic substances in the body. It also generally increases circulation of blood, which in turn strengthens the heart, lungs and kidneys.

No one should just jump into jogging. It is first advisable to have a physical examination to determine the state of one's health. Every person should have a thorough medical check up each year. This is especially true with runners, since they are putting strain on the heart each time they exercise.

One gauge of condition is heart rate. A normal, basic rate for a healthy person is about 72 beats per minute. Exercise can lower heart rate. Most serious distance runners have resting rates well below 40 beats per minute. Even at 80 years of age, Percy's was a healthy 55. Beginning joggers should test their rate from time to time as they progress in their jogging to see if it is lowered.

The daily jogger doesn't need to do a lot of calisthenics before he starts each day. If he uses the five basic movements, he will warm up to running naturally. He should begin with several "stretch-ups" to remove the tension from the body. Then he can switch gears, to walking, ambling, trotting, cantering and, in moments of exhilaration, galloping.

The key is to make running enjoyable, by varying the terrain, pace, distance and movements. The basic movements don't have to be followed in the same order they do for the competitive runner. They can be switched for variety. A jogger could canter at first, break the sequence by trotting, move into a fast gallop, then canter again.

"Hasten slowly," Percy said, "and *feel* your way to fitness and improved health rather than strain your musculature to attain it."

No special clothing is required for jogging, although loose-fitting shirts and shorts are recommended in warm weather and a sweat suit in the cold. When weather is too cold, running should be done indoors, at a recreation center if possible. If the jogger does run outdoors in the very coldest months, he should wear warm sweat clothes, mittens and a wool hat. Some people feel that in the winter months they can substitute basically inactive ways of circulating the blood for jogging. This includes such things as massage and saunas. These are passive forms of circulating the blood and are very inefficient when compared to active forms like jogging.

The jogger should find some accurate way of measuring his runs, either in terms of distance run or amount of time spent running. Rather than map out courses, it is simplest to just use a wrist watch. All running should be on grass or soft surfaces.

CERUTTY'S TRAINING PLAN FOR JOGGERS

Cerutty planned a workout schedule that was designed to help the non-athlete maintain his or her health and fitness and, most important, to help them *stay alive*.

Each day, the person should record his exercise in a training diary, much as a top competitive runner records his workouts. It is also helpful to record one's body weight and pulse each day. The body weight should be recorded at the same time each day, preferably upon rising. Pulse rate should always be taken when the person is in a relaxed state. Daily calorie intake may also be recorded in the same diary.

The schedule Percy devised is flexible. The weight lifting, for instance, shouldn't be done each day. The jogger may already have another regular form of exercise, such as tennis, bicycling or swimming, and if so he needn't do as much of Percy's program. His was designed to give the non-athlete a full blend of needed exercise.

Morning (before breakfast):

1. Five minutes of stretching exercises to wake up the body. This should include walking and stretching-up, the first of the five basic movements.
2. Run in place at a comfortable pace for 3-5 minutes.
3. Do approximately five minutes of sit-ups.
4. Shower.

Work Hours:

If your job is basically sedentary, invent ways of adding exercise.

Lunch Break:

Taking a brisk walk around the block, or just going outside, is a good way of getting some exercise, and it breaks up the monotony of the office.

Afternoon-Evening—(this should precede the evening meal):

1. Five minutes of stretching-up to get rid of the day's tension in the neck, shoulders and back.
2. Weight lifting for 15-20 minutes, using Cerutty's basic lifts. This should occur only two or three times per week at the most, and on days that it does, the run can be shortened.
3. Thirty minutes to an hour of jogging, varying the five movements, as well as running speed and terrain.
4. Do 20-30 sit-ups.
5. Shower.

Everyone has a different work schedule and so this program will apply differently to each person. One general rule is that some activity should separate each meal, and that some light exercise should precede breakfast. This is not only physically sound, it also makes the person more mentally efficient and able.

The benefits of exercise can be counteracted by a lack of attention to other things. Percy cited five points that a jogger should be concerned with: (1)

Australian ultra-distance runner Tony Rafferty has run across that country.

have a complete medical check-up at least once a year; (2) have a moderate intake of all foods, particularly proteins; (3) keep your diet free of chemically processed foods and salts; (4) watch your body weight; (5) abstain from tobacco and alcohol.

These rules largely concern diet, about which many people are careless. They use their exercise as an excuse to eat more and eat worse. They are defeating the purpose of their exercise.

A JOGGER'S DIET

Diet for a jogger is not as strict as for competitive runners. But Cerutty never agreed with what most diet advocates said. He was firmly against *anyone* poisoning his body with unnatural foods.

"Throw the rubbish away," he said, "before the

damn stuff puts *you* away first."

A jogger's diet should not include much protein. "People eat far too much protein," Percy said, "and it is poisoning them." One portion of protein should be eaten to every three portions of carbohydrates, vegetables and fresh fruit.

Table salt should never be added to foods as this is a source of hardening arteries and is unnecessary, anyway.

There are five rules that Percy believed joggers should abide by with regards to jogging:

1. Never drink or eat before exercise. The jogger should allow 3-4 hours after each meal before running. Following practice, a period of at least a half-hour should ensue before eating to allow the body to cool down.

2. No liquids should be drunk with a meal. The last liquid should be consumed a half-hour before eating. Afterwards, the person should wait an hour before drinking.

3. Quantity of food should always be restricted. There should be no between meal snacks, except an occasional piece of fruit.

4. Always avoid eating under stress, amid great noise, while arguing or while angry. The digestive juices cannot do their job when a person is upset.

5. Supplement your diet with vitamins B2 and C. This is especially important if you feel extremely tired after working out.

With regard to the third point, the best way of determining quantity is simply by counting calories. Percy believed that most people should limit their caloric intake to 1200-1600 daily. Of course, this figure varies with the build of a person and the amount of physical work he or she does. Other gauges of whether someone is eating too much are the person's belt notch and the bathroom scales.

If the jogger finds that he is gaining weight when he doesn't want to be, then he should limit himself to two meals a day.

Percy's recommended diet follows:

Breakfast (should be preceded by light exercise):

One cup of tea 30 minutes before the meal.

One or two eggs, soft boiled, poached or scrambled.

One small bowl of assorted fresh fruit that is in season.

A half piece of toast with jam and *no butter.*

No pancakes, waffles or processed cereals. These are dead foods which serve no useful purpose.

Lunch (should be preceded by a walk):

One cup of hot soup.

One bowl of green leafy salad with one teaspoon of dressing oil.

One slice of mild cheese.

No tea, coffee or a dessert is eaten with the lunch.

Dinner (following the afternoon-evening jogging session):

One moderate portion of broiled lean beef, chicken or fish.

One bowl of hot soup.

One large bowl of leafy green salad with vegetables and dressing oil.

A half a baked potato or 10 or less French fries with no salt.

Small equal servings of vegetables and fruit that are in season.

One cup or tea or coffee with light cream and brown sugar can be taken 30 minutes before the main course. A small glass of wine can also be consumed a half-hour before the meal.

One addition that should be made to this discussion of the jogger's diet is the problem of being more tired from exercising and craving more food for energy. Many people actually *gain* weight after they start to exercise. Percy believed this was because they simply weren't eating properly, and also because their exercise was exhausting without being fully beneficial. They weren't using the proper movements and thus weren't getting enough oxygen into their bloodstream.

Adding vitamins to the diet removes much of the tired feeling beginning joggers often feel.

Also, joggers should get 8-10 hours of sleep each night.

PERCY CERUTTY'S RECREATION RUNNING

When he was in his 70s, Percy ran because he liked it and because it kept his body in shape. He didn't do it to compete. So, in many ways, he himself was a recreation runner.

He realized the need for fitness in everyone's life. "Fitness always pays the best dividends in the long run," he told me. "If you have your health, you have everything. For the fit, all things are possible. A fatalistic approach to life is foolish. Man can control his destiny in terms of what he eats, breathes and exercises."

Percy believed that all runners should let their emotions flow out of their body. "Flush out the tensions and pressures of your daily problems," Percy said.

At the age of 80, Cerutty exercised every day at his fitness camp in Portsea. He regularly ran around the training oval outside of his office, occasionally lifted heavy weights and took long walks in the sand along the ocean. It was the beach that had inspired him to write more than 300 poems, many while in his 70s. He also worked frequently in his several vegetable and flower gardens.

"Fitness is the bulwark against the future," he said, and obviously believed.

In his late 70s, Cerutty's diet differed slightly from what he advocated for top athletes, but it was still very health-oriented.

This was a typical day:

Breakfast:

- One cup of weak tea upon rising
- One piece of fresh fruit (apple, banana, orange or a pear) when his body was awakened with some exercise.

Lunch:

- A small glass of wine 30 minutes before the meal.
- Two poached eggs on brown toast or a small portion of raw liver broiled chicken, red salmon, sardines or tuna.
- A half a tomato on a slice of cheese.
- A half a banana.

Dinner:

- A cup of tea or small glass of wine 30 minutes before the meal.
- A moderate portion of broiled beef, lamb, chicken, fish, tuna, raw liver, red salmon or two poached eggs.
- Five or 10 chips with no salt.
- One portion of uncooked vegetables and fresh fruit.

Evening:

- A cup of tea while working in his study.

Percy generally took all liquids while reading or watching the television in his study. He seldom consumed anything while working or while tense, because he believed this led to improper digestion.

Although his program was always directed at the top competitive athlete and he was constantly talking about the potential for lowering records in every event by using the five basic movements, Cerutty was also very aware of running's potential for the average person.

He told me, "Anyone who can run two miles a day can solve his problems at work the next day. 'Dead' men and women do no useful work for the sake of helping humanity."

IV

THE CERUTTY PHILOSOPHY

15

The Stotan Creed

Percy Cerutty's training techniques were just one part of a much larger dream. He often said that when the athletic world fully grasped his ideas, records would be shattered in every event. But his real intention was even more ambitious: to alter the way we think, not only in terms of athletics but in every aspect of living.

His Stotan philosophy (from Stoic and Spartan) was the means of doing this. To say that his philosophical writings, poetry and essays on life were irrelevant to running is a great misconception. In fact, it is because of this feeling that his techniques have not been properly utilized since the time of Herb Elliott.

"I raise the spirits of the athlete," Percy said, "and inspire the soul to a higher state of consciousness. As the athlete grows spiritually as a person, his performance in the physical will gradually unfold to new heights."

Every one of the athletes at Portsea was constantly exposed to his philosphy, and that philosophy provided them with the inspiration and determination to excel. Following his training ideas to improve the body was only half of what Cerutty advocated.

Percy said, "The future, or destiny is a projection of ourselves, and our intrinsic worth! These are nature's absolutes. It is not always the extrinsic and intrinsic drives that determine how great an athlete will become in his event. I say that it is intrinsic *worth.*"

"My Stotan philosophy is based on communication with nature," he said. "This communication takes place when the person sleeps under the stars at night, hears the birds in the morning, feels the sand between his toes, smells the flowers, hears the surf. Nature can bring the mind and body into perfect harmony and balance with the universe. This is one of the factors that allows the athlete to reach new levels of excellence."

What Percy gave to each athlete who came to him (he never recruited) was help in pursuing his destiny. He believed everyone was capable of some form of greatness, but that most neglected to pursue it. In athletics, the forces of nature were an important part of realizing this destiny. He was always opposed to writing training schedules and the regimented style of interval training, which he felt ignored the individual.

"The mastery of the true self," Percy said, "and the refusal to permit others to dominate us is the ultimate in living, and self-expression in athletics. The truly great in any field of endeavor never needed flatteries, adulations or the rewards that are bestowed upon them. To feel a comtempt for the bestower is a concomitant of greatness!"

The idea of pursuing excellence wasn't something Cerutty restricted to athletics. Percy had an uncanny way of recognizing that small spark of greatness that rested in the athletes who came to Portsea to excel in their events.

"All of mankind has something special to contribute for uplifting humanity," Percy said. "Greatness in any field of endeavor is merely a matter of degree, how others appraise us, or how we measure the ascent up the mountain to reach the goal!"

At Portsea, Cerutty accelerated this drive to destiny by immersing his athletes in it full time.

"No one is born great," Percy said. "He may be born to become great. Destiny and fate have a miraculous way of working things out to bring tremendous results."

The fighting spirit that was characteristic of all his top athletes came directly from Cerutty. He gave regular lectures at Portsea and worked individually with each one, inspiring them to work harder, to seek their potential, to be invincible at something.

"The athlete can only become as great as his coach! The person is humble when he listens to what I have to say at my lectures," Percy said, "and then he shows the quality of humility when he faithfully practices the things that I demonstrate so he can excel in his event to reach his maximum potential. Somewhere behind the scenes of a world record-holder, there is always a knowledgeable teacher or coach who has a lot of valuable experience in athletics."

Herb Elliott wrote in his autobiography, "He is like an oasis in the desert of my lost enthusiasm. After listening to him talk, I ran four miles round the track with the galloping action he advocates."

Cerutty was always aware of his tremendous ability to motivate others. When the athlete's personality is expressed through his neural patterns, the person should feel an inner power that surges through every cell in his body while he is competing in his event.

"At all my lectures and demonstrations," he said, "I inspire the athletes with my poetry and essays. Then, each one of the athletes go in a separate direction to be along to practice what he has heard, to clean the venom out of his system!"

He lectured his athletes on all aspects of life and sport. Some of the athletes who trained at "Ceres" worked harder than the others, and this is why they excelled further to set world records. Destiny is on the side of the hard worker who never gives up until the goal is achieved. Those individuals open their own doors in life and sport.

"To be great in any event in track and field," Percy said, "the person's life must be a masterpiece like a great work of art."

It bothered Percy that most people seemed so afraid to let their personalities stand naked, that so many people clung to secret hopes and dreams that would never surface, and which would only cause anxiety and frustration. People are much more energetic and ambitious, he believed, when they find an outlet for their emotions. For the athletes at Portsea, that outlet was running, jumping and throwing. For most people, the outlet is never found.

Lack of immediate success is the most common reason why people give up their goals. But failure should always be looked upon positively, not negatively.

"If an athlete wants to be an Olympic champion, he must cleave to his destiny, and work hard until he achieves his goal. When the person works hard each day, he will find the way that will bring him one step closer to satisfying his goals. Thought is born from failure! Only when the person's actions fail to satisfy his basic needs is there grounds for serious thought. The greater the failure, the more soul-searching that is needed for success in the future," Percy said.

Success should never be gauged just in terms of records or victories. Success should be measured by how much the person enjoys what he is doing and to what degree he is striving to do his best.

"Success shows what can be done!" Percy said. "What has been done! Failure creates a lot of serious dedication for the future. Never be seriously disappointed with your minor setbacks when you are training and competing. Most things tend to work out in the athlete's favor in the long run."

All of the Cerutty world record-holders reached their maximum potential that destiny would allow. After studying with Cerutty, I found that athletics is never an egotistical fantasy. The person who is destined to become an Olympic champion truly believes that all things are possible.

Cerutty leads the charge up Portsea's famous sandhill, an important place for his strength training.

"When you have done your level best at anything in life and sport," Percy said, "leave it at that! It is then that God has a chance to step in and take over to bring out the best results."

Because most people are not actively engaged in a quest for excellence, they often ask the runner, "Why do you run?" Percy thought it was futile to explain to, or even associate for any length of time with, a person who wastes his time. Anyone who has a burning desire to achieve his goals in life and sport will only have his desires dulled if he spends too much time with idlers.

"You have to work hard to win," Cerutty said. "You can't win if you don't start doing something about your goal right now. Success and achievement awaits he who can grasp it. If the athlete wants to become an Olympic champion, he must work hard at his event, even if it means working for years to reach the goal. Work does things. Hard things take time to do. Impossible things take a little longer. *Patience* and *persistence* are the key words to success in athletics. There is never any hurry on the creative plane!"

Percy was not quite as regimented as he often sounded. Although he believed everyone should always try to reach their full potential, he thought they also needed some fun in the process. He encouraged his athletes to wrestle, frolic and surf at the beach when they weren't running.

"In spite of his rough, brusque manner, he's a kind warm-hearted soul," Elliott said in *The Golden Mile*.

The more familiar picture of Percy Cerutty was of his ceaseless dedication to inspiring others and to improving himself in the process.

The solution is to construct a positive environment around your goal that prevents the intrusion of distracting influences. This is what Percy did at Portsea. He literally created a natural environment, built on positive influences, and so those that stayed at the camp for long periods of time all became successful. Percy's ideas were what inspired his athletes, and unlike the ideas that are read in a book and soon diminish, his always remained strong because he was constantly recharging his athletes with them.

Herb Elliott said, "Percy helped me to world records not so much by improving my technique, but by releasing the soul power in my mind that I only vaguely thought existed. He is an emotional person who is able to harness emotion and transfer it to another person."

It should always be remembered that Percy was not just a coach of athletics; he was a philosopher and a poet who inspired athletes to reach their full potential.

About the Author

Larry Myers is a graduate of Adams State College in Colorado where he received an educational degree in English and physical education. While in college, he competed in all the weight events. He later taught in the Denver Public Schools and competed for the Colorado Track Club, winning a Rocky Mountain AAU title in the hammer throw.

In 1973, Myers went to Portsea, Australia to study under Percy Cerutty at the International Athletic Center. When he returned to the United States a year later, Myers gave a lecture tour with Cerutty in California.

Myers currently resides in Denver, Colo., where he teaches Cerutty's athletic techniques and philosophy. He is also at work on a second book, about George Hackenschmidt and Arthur Newton.